Converting your books to ebooks with InDesign CC

I0411132

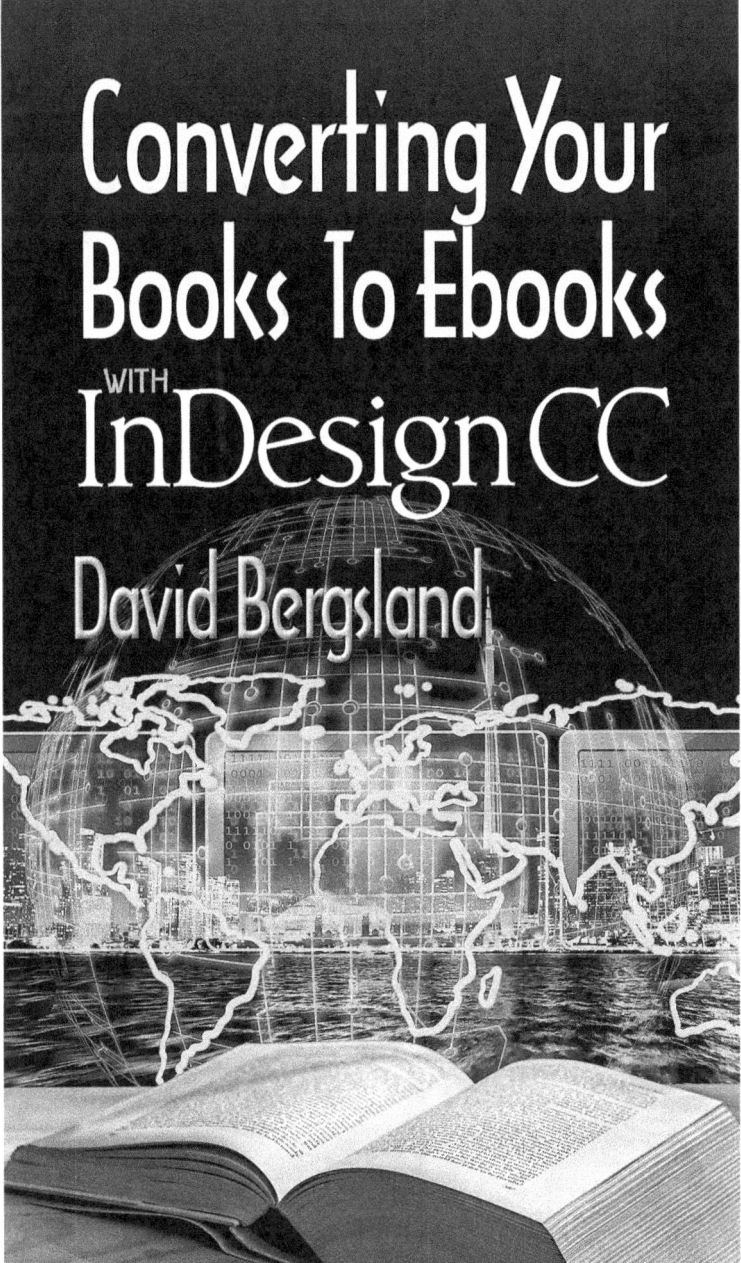

Converting Your Books To Ebooks

WITH InDesign CC

David Bergsland

Written and published in Fall, 2016
© David Bergsland • All Rights Reserved
ISBN-13: 978-1537645384
ISBN-10: 1537645382

Mankato, Minnesota • http://radiqx.com
info@radiqx.com

Please let us know if there is anyway I can help
you in your publishing endeavors.

This is dedicated to my friends and readers who help keep me on track with their postings, comments, and reviews. I wouldn't get better at my craft nearly as quickly without the ones the Lord sends along side to help me. I'm grateful!

Contents

There are several assumptions in this book

This is a design book, not a set of software tutorials. The ebook conversion process is at the tail end of the book production workflow.

The two main assumptions are:

🐫 **First, that you have used InDesign CC:** I'm not expecting power-user-level experience. But, you do know how to make a book using paragraph, character, object and table styles to globally control the formatting

🐫 **Second, that you have designed your book in print:** You know basic typography and professional formatting. Your book is fully formatted, and now you need to make an ebook conversion.

If you not have a fully formatted print version, you'll need to set up your ebook from scratch

That process is beyond the scope of this little book. These topics are covered thoroughly in my other books about publishing books. They include my various versions of:

🐫 *Book Publishing With InDesign CC:* This is my latest book on the subject.

🐫 *Writing In InDesign:* There are at least four editions covering the use of InDesign as a writing tool in the various versions, and the vast benefits of working fully formatted as your book progresses.

🐫 *Basic Typography:* This is just the typography sections of the book production books.

These all cover font usage and paragraph design—which you need to know before you begin formatting. Knowledge of paragraph design, especially, is crucial to building a book which is easy to read and comfortable in the hand of the reader.

Although this part of book production is rarely discussed, typography applied to paragraph design and page layout enables you to produce a book which your readers will find easy and comfortable to read and understand.

It's all about the readers!

Laying the foundation

As I get started, I want to say that this is a professional workflow for authors and books doing the full publishing routine of print, Kindle, iBooks, Kobo, Nook, and all the rest. Before the choruses rise up in defense of other workflows, let me tell you my reasonings.

I fully recognize that most people write in Word and many produce their ebooks in Word. Many more code their ebooks by hand in HTML and CSS. What these people do not realize [in most cases] is this simple fact starts their book under a great handicap. Many of the very effective typographic tools for communication are simply missing, If they are publishing their own book, Word simply does not provide many of the best tools for communicating clearly and easily with their readers.

I begin my ebook conversions with a fully formatted book—the print version or the downloadable PDF

These versions allow me to develop the typography of the book and have the most tools to communicate clearly and comfortably with the reader. The key is that all portions of the book: paragraphs, tables, and graphics must be formatted with styles. Only this will give you the global control of the book you need to make effective conversions for the various distributors like Lightning source, Createspace, Lulu, Kindle KDP, the iBooks Store, NookPress, Kobo Writing Life, Smashwords, Draft2Digital, Scribd, Gumroad, and so on. The entire process is covered in *Book Publishing with InDesign CC.* This book is concerned with the conversion to the various ebook formats: downloadable color PDFs, ePUBs—both fixed layout and reflowable, with and without embedded fonts, and the adjustments necessary to make your ePUBs convert well to Kindle books.

Books are not entirely about words

Of course as a writer this may not make much sense to you. But please hear me out. For years I have taught graphic designers that the content is all that matters. Now I am teaching writers that presentation and layout are a big part of your book. For designers, this has been a major fight because many never read the copy they design into books and printed materials. Now I am dealing with writers who do not see the need for typography and layout skills.

Most designers do not deal well with words

Graphic designers [and this includes most book designers] are visual people, focused on how things look. One of my major concerns as I started to write books in the mid-1990s was my experience in my digital publishing classes using published textbooks only as bad examples providing poor communication. As a pastor, commercially available Bible studies were just as bad. They were normally almost impossible to read or use—being more focused on style than communication. The examples are endless.

My pursuit of functional, reader-centered books has been fraught with trials. I was constantly bumping up against standardized procedures of traditional publishers which really made their books hard to read or use effectively. This focus on the reader is so far outside the norm in publishing today that there is little room for an author who even cares about these things (except in this brand new world of on-demand self-publishing).

Let's talk about some simple examples of this lack of concern for the reader

🐄 **Illustrations listed by number with no connection to the copy which talks about what is illustrated:** Most traditional non-fiction publishers require this typographic horror. In many cases, authors are not allowed to even pick out the images because they are not considered professional enough to understand what is required for a graphic.

The results are illustrations, maps, charts, and photos listed by number which are often not on the same page (or even the same chapter) as the content they illustrate. *Why bother to even have them?* Few readers will find them or take the time to look for them. The result is frustrated readers who simply quit reading in disgust.

For fiction, it is equally bad to have an illustration or map which cannot be easily referenced by the reader. In my novels I add maps where they are needed in the copy to help the reader understand what is going on. Remember, the goal is to assist the reader. For ebooks, I am giving each important map a chapter head in the Table of Contents.

🐄 **Heads and subheads generated by designers:** In many cases over the years I spent as a graphic designer, I wrote all the subheads, developed all the lists, wrote all the captions, and even wrote most of the headlines.

I developed them out of a need to help direct the reader through the copy I was formatting. The author commonly had no clue that they were desirable or necessary. I formatted them as a service to the reader. But I was a real minority as mentioned. Many designers do not even read the copy they lay out, as I said.

As a writer, you must be aware of these issues and realize that they are a primary method of clearing up communication with the reader. Heads, subheads, list design, and all the rest are key elements of your support of easy understanding by the reader.

Page layout determined by fashion and visual concerns: In the graphic design world, fonts are often chosen because they look good. Layouts are determined by fashion. Columns, margins, sidebars and the like are chosen to stimulate visual interest and provoke excitement instead of being chosen to communicate the content effectively, clearly, and accessibly. Clarity and accuracy are rarely considered.

The most glaring example of this is seen in the books where content is broken up into small pieces—supposedly to help people with short attention spans. We recently bought a creationism book that is virtually unreadable. The gorgeous, fancy illustrations push the copy into bits and pieces that are lost in the visual clutter of the pages' backgrounds. My wife gave up on it and asked me for a verbal report.

But it goes much further than that. Here's a quote from Wikipedia about the normal traditional editorial process (I realize it is difficult to read):

> "*(Once)* a decision is taken to publish a work, and the technical legal issues resolved, the author may be asked to improve the quality of the work through rewriting or smaller changes, and the staff will edit the work. Publishers may maintain a house style, and staff will copy edit to ensure that the work matches the style and grammatical requirements of each market. Editors often choose or refine titles and headlines. Editing may also involve structural changes and requests for more information."

Notice that there is nothing here about serving the readers. Publishers will normally insist that you fit your content into their style—even if that style hinders your book and may even offend your readers. The readers' needs are not part of the process. It's all about sales and the marketing decisions of the publisher. The reader's needs seldom take priority.

Books are not entirely about design either

As an author/publisher, or simply a book designer, book design is a tool to help the reader easily follow the content written by the author. The goal is to make concepts and explanations easy to read and locate, comfortably presented in a manner in which the reader can grasp and retain the content. Yes, that's a tall order, but it's at the core of book writing, design, and production in all the various versions needed to day.

You must learn
to produce your own books.

For the past two decades, I have taught digital publishing skills. During that time I have written and published books, both traditionally and on-demand. I have taught skills to present digital content transparently, effectively, and gracefully.

But, Word [and word processors in general] cannot do this. There are skills and capabilities that are necessary which are simply not available in Office. It is true, that ePUBs and Kindle books cannot do many of these things either. But unless you know about typography and have developed the skill to produce reading excellence, your ebooks will not be pleasant experiences for your readers—they will not recommend your books.

Quality levels required for professional publishing

- 🐄 **Typography:** The skill to use fonts, paragraph styling, and page layout to invisibly communicate content: point size, leading, small caps, ligatures, oldstyle figures, lining figures, ems, ens, discretionary hyphens, tracking, kerning, and much more. All of these things are controlled with styles: paragraph, character, and object. For this you need a professional page layout program. Many of these things are not yet available in ePUBs unless you use specialized fonts.

- 🐄 **High resolution, full-color images:** You want vector graphics if possible. Printing requires 300 dpi minimum for photos and bitmapped images. You'll need Photoshop for the high resolution images. They need to be PDFs, EPSs, AIs, PSDs, or TIFFs for printing quality work. For ePUBs you'll be using color and the highest resolutions possible on a practical level. JPEGs, GIFs, and PNGs are necessary, but FXL images work better at 150 dpi.

Covers must be created at high resolution to enable all the various sizes required by Apple, Amazon, B&N, and so on. Kindle is currently requesting that "For best quality, your image would be 2820 pixels on the shortest side and 4500 pixels on the longest side" for the JPEGs uploaded for your Kindle books. That is a very large image: 9.4" x 15" at 300 dpi—plus it is not in the normal 600x800 size ratio which has been recommended for ePUB images.

🐄 **Page layout:** A thorough understanding of columns, margins, alignments, indents, gutters, lists, tables, headlines, subheads, sidebars, running heads, drop caps, and much more is required. Just a simple sidebar with a text wrap around the overlapping portions of copy is much more complex in a reflowable ePUB even though it is a simple thing in an ePUB FXL or downloadable PDF..

Some of you already know quite a bit of this—if you've been using InDesign before. But, to produce a professional book of excellent quality these things must be taken into account. Yes, much of this applies to your ebook designs also.

Writing and editing in InDesign gives you layout power

Until you've tried it, you will find it hard to imagine the power of writing/editing fully formatted. You can see the page as it develops and adjust things to help the reader understand your points. You really can help the reader comprehend the message. That's what excellent book design is all about. Even if you're just formatting already written material, typographic book design matters.

You can use a subhead for clarity, a kicker as a small lead-in style to emphasize a header, lists to recapture the reader's attention with their rhythmic order, a sidebar for peripheral information to entertain the good readers, a table for overly complex lists, and much more.

Even more important, you can add graphics and illustration in the midst of the content which talks about the content of that artwork. Charts, graphics, closeups, diagrams, and info-graphics can be an immense help to your readers.

This is where page layout apps like InDesign truly shine. Photoshop is part of the package. Plus, InDesign can produce graphics faster and often better than specialized illustration apps like Illustrator.

You will be able see on the page, as you write, edit, and put the book together, how clearly the content is being communicated—or not. It helps you change your content into something that communicates clearly and easily to your readers. It lets you see boring areas and fix them as you write. It provides the control you need to speak to your specific niche—emphasizing unique niche concepts as you go. You can also see when you've gone too far and lapsed into mere busyness and clutter.

Basically formatting in a page layout program gives you tools that word processors have a hard time even imagining—which could not be accomplished in that glorified typewriter even if you perceived the need. You will learn to communicate much more clearly. You'll focus on the readers more easily and on what you can do to help them. You can actually try to put yourself in the readers' shoes and answer their questions using both the content and the layout.

Reality orientation

But let's face it, beginning authors don't normally have the foresight to do something like this—in most cases. By the time you are considering doing something like what we are discussing, you have commonly published a book or more. If you are just starting out, the good news is that books like this will show you what you need to do to produce excellent books. It takes time to learn how to write, how to communicate clearly, how to convert the vision you've been given, plus the actual nuts and bolts required to work in reality. This is grown-up work (no matter what your actual physical age is).

Plus, there is a lot to learn: typography, page layout, printing limitations, ebook limitations, and much more. BUT! You can do it simply, line upon line, precept upon precept, as you grow into the publisher you need to be.

 Remember: My assumption is that you already know typography and page layout. If not, read the *Basic Assumptions* on page ix. This book just shows you how to convert your fully format-ted book into an ebook.

How long will it take?

That depends on how seriously you take the work of book production. I used to teach this in two intense semesters to people starting from scratch who were not interested in writing. Most just wanted to draw. As a writer this will come more easily.

You can be up and running in a week or so, competent in a matter of months, and producing excellent work within a year.

But you will need to work at it and practice. In this new publishing paradigm, we can publish blog postings, white papers, books, booklets, essays, teachings, Bible studies, prophecies, forecasts, guides, novels, press releases, media kits, and more. Of course, this is all digital production.

So, you need a good computer. The main thing is that ebooks are so new that current software is required. This requires a relatively new computer. What I am listing as minimums are based on the assumption that you will be using the Creative Cloud apps. At the least, you'll need InDesign CC. This is especially true for ebooks for fixed layout ePUB export just began there. For Photoshop, CS4 or better will work.

Computer minimums YES, MOST OF YOU KNOW THIS

- 🐄 **You really need a Mac:** but I won't argue about it. You'll need a 64-bit Intel CPU or better, a monitor at least 1600 pixels wide [2000 pixels or more is better], 8 GB or more of RAM [but you really need 16 GB], Mac OSX.10 or better [Windows 7 or better], a 300 GB hard drive or better, and safe backup storage.

- 🐄 **You'll need a full extended keyboard with a numerical keypad and the editing keys:** If you have a laptop with all its limitations, you'll want a wired USB or Bluetooth keyboard with a full set of function keys, editing keys, and a

numerical keypad. It will really slow you down
if you are working with a limited keyboard.

The numerical keypad is essential for style shortcuts and the editing keys are necessary for easy
navigation through your book: You will really
slow your production speed and you'll not like
InDesign without the full keyboard. It's needed
for custom shortcuts, and many of the standard
ones like page navigation.

If you already have a PC: you can use it providing
it meets the criteria above. Plus you'll need to be
able to calibrate your monitor.

These are all minimums. You'll actually want the
16 GB RAM to keep working at speed and to
avoid crashes. Each book will add at least a large
portion of a Gigabyte into storage. So a 500-1000
GB hard drive is not out of line at all.

**You'll also need high-speed internet and
a PostScript printer for proofing:** You will
be uploading and downloading PDFs that
are often dozens of megabytes in size,
commonly many times in a day. It often
cannot be done at all with a slow internet
connection. You will also be doing all your
marketing online and you do not want
to be wasting time with slow access.

For ePUB proofs I recommend an iPad as the
best quality ereader and the most versatile,
Android tablets will work, but for Kindle proofs a
Fire really helps.

InDesign CC, but CS5 is fine for the rest: You'll want InDesign CC, at least, at $20 a month. But the full CC package is only $50 a month. Actually, you can get by with CS4 or even CS3 for Illustrator, Photoshop, and the rest, but you need InDesign CC. Every version does substantially better ePUBs and fixed layout ePUBs require CC.

Get the non-profit or academic versions: (if you qualify). A good resource for these discounts and information on whether you qualify or not is found at the AcademicSuperstore Website. They just need a valid school ID or a scan of your non-profit paperwork, certificate, or whatever. Yes, it is worth taking an accredited class to access academic pricing. Remember, learning to produce your own books will save you $500 to $2000 for every book published. Publishing even two books a year will cover your software expenses.

Except for InDesign, you can buy old versions from eBay and other similar venues: You will need InDesign, Photoshop, and Acrobat Pro—at a minimum.

In this field you must keep up

Because of all the changes coming with HTML5, CSS3, and ePUB3 you'll need to keep current software. Plus, make sure you have a computer which can handle the new versions. I had to buy a new computer to work with CS5 back in 2009. You need to plan on a new PC computer every couple of years. Macs last quite a bit longer. My old computer still runs fine. My wife is using it. But I can no longer use it for my work. I was forced to get a new computer in 2014 with 16 GB RAM primarily because of MacOS changes and to work with video. But notice that I got five years out of the old one and it still works fine for everything but book production. It's hard to beat the iMac. It's designed for people like us.

Page layout basics

Setting up your book to be read: One of the more daunting aspects of book design for the inexperienced is page layout. Most people have Word experience and as I have said countless times already—Word cannot do professional page layout. In fact, it is worse than that because Word's attempts give you bad habits and poor expectations—which must be corrected. This costs you both time and money.

Many settings have to be covered for every document. Many of these are set up as you go through the Preferences in InDesign. Every application has important decisions to be made in Preferences. To repeat, the point is to set up your applications so they work best for you. But all I can really do for Word users is tell you to keep it simple and consistent using styles so that the conversion to InDesign is faster and easier. Yes, ebooks require fully formatted content as the bare beginning.

Before I get started with this, I need remind you of the goal: *a beautiful book which is comfortable to read.*

You need a customized set of styles to enable you to keep your book consistent and give you global control over the entire book as you format. Excellent typography is only possible if you understand how to design paragraphs. Styles make paragraph design possible. We will deal with them conceptually, but you should know this is why InDesign is so good. These options often step outside the entire paradigm of a word processor.

Designing your paragraphs

I need to share a little about setting up your paragraphs. Most of this knowledge is assumed by software manuals and publishing Websites [yes, this is true of InDesign documentation also]. Somehow they seem to believe that your little psyche will be stifled if any opinion on normalcy is mentioned—or some such idiocy. It's not magic or luck when you produce reading materials that are enjoyable to read. It is the result of setting your copy up (formatting it) in a manner that the reader instantly recognizes and comfortably understands.

You must lead the reader through your writing effortlessly—completely unaware of your guidance. You need to make your writing feel natural, comfortable, and obvious to help the reader receive the content.

 My way is not the only way: As I go through this little presentation, I will be simply sharing what I use. My hope is that you can look at my usage for conceptual understanding. Then convert that for your use. I will attempt to give you the arguments that have convinced me to do things in this manner. But, there is no right or wrong (once you are inside the relatively wide parameters of normalcy).

In our modern culture, huge numbers of people have difficulty reading. People often know how to read (technically) but they hate to actually do it. I've heard stats as high as 60% of Americans are functionally illiterate. Most people agree it is a huge percentage even if it is as low as a third of adults. They may be able to read [literate in the polls], but it is difficult for them, in a second language, or they just hate reading [so in practice they rarely or never read]. I know many young men and women (fifty years old or less) who avoid reading entirely [or as much as possible]—even though they are considered fully literate by polls and testing. Many have college degrees.

The need for comfort

The result is that we must go out of our way to make our books accessible to poor readers. Reading is hard to avoid. But many do. We have a large and growing portion of our middle class who get all of their information from social media, TV, movies, and videos.

Modern interactive features: This is an area you need to thoroughly examine. My opinion is that adding video and such to a book changes it into something entirely different. The non-reader may be more attracted to the video content, BUT would they ever buy a "book" in the first place? If you feel the need for video, you should consider whether you actually need a "book" at all.

We can argue all we want about these media options and their limited amount of actual content. But, this fact remains: even those who buy our books may well have trouble reading.

We must help them as much as we can with our formatting and layout. We must be kind to our readers—gentle and loving. If our readers experience any discomfort or reading difficulty we have probably lost them. They will simply not finish reading our content. This must become your basic, bottom line focus for your book designs.

I am a very good and very fast reader. Yet I simply put books aside that are difficult to read—unless the content is required or very compelling. I am not talking about difficult content (though that can be a problem). I am talking about poor layouts, columns that are too wide, fonts that are too stylized, overly busy layouts, and all the rest.

As mentioned, a while back I was struggling with a book on creationism. My wife had given up and asked me to brief her on it when I finished reading it. The content is exciting. The layout is so poor with photographic backgrounds, glossy paper, excessive line lengths and a host of other problems—I had to force myself to read it. The only difference with me is that I am tuned into this problem so I often notice when I do this with a book. Most people are not conscious of why they put down a book. They simply do not read it.

The poetry filter

Here's another example. I wonder how many of you are like me? I probably shouldn't admit this, but anything in a book which is formatted as poetry I skip (except in scripture). I simply pass over that portion of the copy and continue on. My experience over the years is that the content in poetry is very limited and far too open to interpretation. I am almost always looking for facts—easily accessible facts. In a novel, I am looking for plot and character development. Poetry has never provided this for me. So, I have developed reading habits that keep me from wasting time. I jump to the explanation of the poetry that inevitably follows.

I am sure this horrifies many of you. I am not saying that this poetry filter of mine is good or desirable. I am simply saying that it exists. Again, the only thing strange is that *[as an author, typographer, and book designer]* I am more aware of my reading habits—so I noticed this behavior.

What reading filters do you have? More importantly, what reading filters do your readers have? You need to know: I suspect you need to examine yourself. It's hard to say what you have been missing all these years. We all have things we just do not read—often for subconscious reasons. As typographers we try to limit those reactions. At the very least, we need to be aware of possible issues.

For example, in one of the author groups of which I am a member, we had an extended argument about the amount of description needed in a novel. It appeared that, in general, the younger the reader the less important they considered description to be. The older the reader, again generally speaking, the more they thought excellent descriptions kept books from feeling thin, less weighty, or underdeveloped.

The best way to find out what's available is in styles

In InDesign, virtually anything that is possible to do to a paragraph is available. So, to talk about the typography of paragraphs we need to go through the options available in paragraph and character styles. This will show you some or many things you had no idea were even possibilities.

To repeat: In this book, I am skipping this with the assumption that you already know these materials. If you do not, you need to learn what is necessary; what is possible; what works, and, most importantly, what improves readability. In *Book Publishing With InDesign CC* I have 190 pages covering this basic knowledge to get you up and running.

Book production

Let's start with a brief review of the process to make sure we are on the same page: Again, this is a very complex process. It is not particularly difficult, but the procedure is certainly not simple. This is subject to fashion, but be careful. Much of this is about the print version.

The book production process

Get the vision: You start with your idea. You research the market and try to determine your niche. This is an area fraught with uncertainty, because you really have no idea if it will sell or who will buy it. Even free books need to be positioned to attract readers looking for your specific content.

Pick a size: This again is more complicated than it looks and largely applies to print. But in another way it is no real problem. Anything you choose to start with can easily be reformatted to another size once everything is in place and completely controlled by styles. When in doubt start with a 6×9 page for print. For your ePUBs, I recommend a 6" X9.6" page for fixed layout and a 600x800 pixel text frame for reflowable.

You need to pray about this or at least seriously think about it. Many times I have been led to a specific size to use for a particular book. Remember who is going to use your book. Know the demographics of your future (and commonly unknown to you as yet) group of readers—your niche. Often it will surprise you once you actually begin selling your book.

 For InDesign, you need to plan things out a bit: You will eventually have many different formats and page sizes. I am just using a Primary Text Frame and doing my additional formats individually. I find I usually need to write new copy or produce new graphics—especially for the ePUBs and Kindle versions where special fonts don't work well and the graphics need to be so radically converted.

I used to always start with print and write for all formats. More recently (as I am doing for this book), I am starting with the downloadable PDF and building the other versions off of it—because the graphics are all in color there.

🐄 **Using your personal set of default styles, begin writing or adding pieces:** All you do is type Command+Num6 (or whatever shortcut you use for your headline style) and start writing. If you are using pieces from essays, blog posts, booklets or whatever else you have written to be a part of this, just paste them in order and format as you go.

🐄 **If you are using Word:** Place the Word doc into InDesign and reformat it into your styles. The styles from Word are missing too much to use effectively.

🐄 **You need to keep these styles fluid in your mind:** One of the real blessings of using styles is that you can develop your book style over the first few chapters. There will be a real ebb and flow as you adjust your styles—especially your paragraph spacing—as you watch the pages come together.

Front matter & back matter

You need to add your front and back matter as you are putting the book together. You need to be thinking about the entire package throughout the writing and production of the book. There are several (often many) pages of materials that need to be at the front and back of your book. Many of them are optional. Several are not.

Some are required for print but not used for ebooks. For example, in print, you must have a title page and a copyright page. You almost certainly need a Table of Contents (the actual type should not be in an ebook though the setup must be done). You may or may not need an introduction, a dedication, or any of about a dozen other possibilities. You should have an index for non-fiction The following is deeply indebted to Wikipedia and the volunteer writers and editors who have spent so much time putting information like this together.

Front matter choices

- **Advertising blurbs and testimonials:** This would include lists of additional books by the author and quotes from reviewers. I know they are commonplace, but they are certainly gauche.

  Though this is merely my opinion, such self-aggrandizing always seems a bit desperate and is bragging at best (be it on your head).

- **Half Title:** This page just has the title—no subtitle, author name, or anything else. It is the first page inside the cover. You normally use the title font and style from the cover, but smaller. Not used in ePUBs.

🐄 **Frontispiece:** This is an illustration on the page facing the title page.

An old German title page with frontispiece from 1722 AD [WIKIMEDIA COMMONS].

As you can see above, this can be a very stylish and elegant way to start your book. If done well, it offers comfort and tradition to your book design. You should consider this. But it's difficult to use in Reflowable ePUBs. Downloadable PDFs and ePUB FXL versions need readers' spreads.

🐄 **Title page:** In print, this page is commonly a reduced version of your book cover in grayscale, unless you use a frontispiece. Ideally the title page shows the title of the work, the person or group responsible for its intellectual content, the place & year of publication, and the name of the publisher. For ePUBs you use the 600x800 cover.

🐄 **Copyright page:** This is normally on the back of the title page. Some would say that it is absolutely required to be there. It contains copyright owner name and the year, the publishing staff, edition and printing information, ISBN, cataloging details for the Library Of Congress. The lawyers love this page in a big publishing house. Hopefully, we are more merciful than that.

🐄 **Table of contents:** This is built and updated with the Table of Contents... command at the bottom of the Layout menu. It's powerful and I have a tendency to add too much. I am in the process of rethinking my TOC use. I'm moving smaller subhead content to the index. But it works well in print, downloadable PDF, and ePUBs. In the ebooks, the entries even have live links to the indicated copy.

🐄 **List of figures:** This is more needed for fine art books than anything, but this would be the place it goes. It is also produced with the TOC commands. You'll need special paragraph styles for your captions which can then be collected.

🐄 **List of tables:** If your book is data-driven, this might be a good service for your readers. This is also produced with the TOC commands. You'll need special paragraph styles for your table headers which can then be collected.

🐄 **Dedication:** This where you name the people whose inspiration enabled you to write the book. In ebooks, it's usually at the end of the book.

- 🐄 **Acknowledgments:** These are all the people, groups, and Websites who helped you. In ebooks, it's usually at the end of the book.

- 🐄 **Foreword:** This is written by a real person, other than yourself.

- 🐄 **Preface:** This covers the story of how the book came into being, or how the idea for the book was developed. It often includes the acknowledgments.

- 🐄 **Introduction:** Here you can give the purpose, goals, and organization of your book. This is where you tell the reader the devices you use throughout the book [like little graphics for tips, how you will identify sources, and things like that].

- 🐄 **Prologue:** Written by the narrator or a character in the book, this gives the setting and background details, some earlier story that ties into this book, or other relevant details. It sets the stage for the real content.

Many of these things are not necessary or even desirable for all books. You need to be careful that you don't bore the reader into tears—to the place where they simply put the book down because it is too much trouble to get to the actual content of the book. [Which is why they bought the book in the first place, remember?]

Back matter choices

There are many options here also. These are more reader services and references to help them as they read your book. Where much of the front matter helps fiction, the back matter is almost entirely for non-fiction. Of course, Tolkien loved to add back matter about Middle Earth—which further developed the reality of his fictional world.

It's all up to you: However, if you ignore all of these things, the reader might well feel the book is not complete.

Epilogue: This is a great service to the reader in fiction. For me and my wife anyway, we often talk about books that just dump you off with many of the issues unresolved. We want completion, a sense that we know what happened and that it's all OK.

To quote from Wikipedia:

"An epilogue is a final chapter at the end of a story that often serves to reveal the fates of the characters. Some epilogues may feature scenes only tangentially related to the subject of the story. They can be used to hint at a sequel or wrap up all the loose ends. They can occur at a significant period of time after the main plot has ended. In some cases, the epilogue has been used to allow the main character a chance to 'speak freely'. An epilogue can continue in the same narrative style and perspective as the preceding story, although the form of an epilogue can occasionally be drastically different from the overall story."

Afterword: "When the author steps in and speaks directly to the reader, that is more properly considered an afterword."

Conclusion: This is also called a summary or a synopsis.

Appendix/Addendum: This contains additional materials to flesh out a particular portion of the book. You should consider this option as a reader service. As Appendices they can work really well. But, they can also be released as separate booklets for readers of earlier editions and for more advanced readers who might otherwise skip your book.

🐄 **Glossary:** Relevant word definitions

🐄 **Bibliography:** Books used and additional readings

🐄 **Index:** Word and phrase references by page

🐄 **Errata:** No longer needed for on-demand publishing. We simply upload a revised version.

🐄 **Colophon:** "With the development of the private press movement from around 1890, colophons became conventional in private press books, and often included a good deal of additional information on the book, including statements of limitation, data on paper, ink, type and binding, and other technical details. Some such books include a separate 'Note about the type', which will identify the names of the primary typefaces used, provide a brief description of the type's history and a brief statement about its most identifiable physical characteristics." [Wikipedia]

This is just a fun addition, especially for a book like this that is about book production.

Hopefully, you've been thinking about these things

The appropriate time to add front matter and back matter is during the writing of the book. A passage may suggest an appendix. For example, as I was editing in my *Writing In InDesign* book, I noticed that it was really confusing to refer the reader to my Website to get the instructions to add the basic paragraph styles with which to start your use of them. It seemed good to add the step-by-step for a basic set of styles to my books.

Concern for reader confusion may lead to a prologue to ease them into the main story or content. Mainly you need to be aware that all of these other things exist. Then you will develop them in process while you are writing. It's not good to start dealing with them after everything is written. Often you've forgotten the incidents that will trigger good reader service content like this.

Again! It's all about the reader

Continuously, you must consider how to serve the reader. You are writing for them. They deserve all the help you can give them. Often you must radically shift things to make things better.

For example, in my verse by verse Bible studies it finally dawned on me that I was raising an almost impenetrable barrier to reading the book. I had an introduction/prologue that included doctrinal statements, a short testimony (it grew with each book), and more. The short testimony of my spiritual walk at the front of the book finally grew to over a half dozen pages and was keeping the readers from reaching the real content. So, I changed it to a reference in the introduction and moved it to an afterword in the back matter.

In fact, for a while I moved much of this material to the back of many of my books in multiple appendices. I leave a brief listing of the appendixes available and then go on with the main part of the book. I did this to give the reader easier access to the real content. Try to watch yourself as you read other books to see what you find irritating.

Excessive front matter

This is especially true of ebooks. This is where I first actually noticed the problem. Front matter is really jarring there. There is really no comfortable way to flip pages and skip to the actual content in an ebook. So you want to get the reader there quickly. I have eliminated or moved all the front matter in all my ebooks except for a very brief copyright statement and the dedication.

But there is no right or wrong here. You need to determine what your reader would like. You might ask them in your blog. For sure, ask your reviewers. Make sure you have people from your target audience doing your reviews. Above all do not use these devices to "bulk up"your book. That's a subtle form of fraud. If the content is not necessary, do not add it to your book.

The need for features of the book will become apparent as you are writing. In this brief book I'm avoiding more of the background and simply trying to set you up so you have the knowledge you need to get started with ePUBs.

All of InDesign's output is an ebook

As you know, almost all of InDesign's output is in ebook form. Even for the print book, we produce a PDF. This PDF reads wonderfully well in iBooks or any ereader which can handle PDFs. However, even that PDF should really be modified for excellent use as a downloadable PDF. The graphics can all be in color, for example.

Now that ePUBs and Kindle books have reached the tipping point [become more than 50% of sales for most self-publishers], we truly need to be sure we make a excellent ebook for sale. At this point, my best sales are again through Createspace [Amazon's print service]. But this is changing fairly quickly. Both the iBookstore and Kobo are growing even faster than Kindle. Nook is shooting itself in the foot.

I've almost completely quit using the KDP Select option which allows me to offer the book for free by giving Amazon exclusivity for three months or more. *[There is one exception I'll mention later.]* The free option *[use with KDP Select for promotions]* doesn't seem to work well for anyone other than writers of romances or more distasteful genre like erotica, horror, and so on. It's a marketing consideration.

Basically we need to learn to be fluid on these things. There are new startups [almost weekly] trying to break the monopoly Amazon now stakes out on a pure ease of shopping and book discovery level. As soon as one of them gains traction [Tomely, Draft2Digital, Book-Shout, and at least a dozen more today], book selling will go to the next level. Draft2Digital has done well, and I normally use it instead of Smashwords, at this point. We desperately need an excellent shopping service for ebooks. Overall, outside of Amazon, the ebook shopping experiences are still at a very rudimentary level.

InDesign is currently the best WYSIWYG production software for ebooks

There is still a long ways to go, but there is a good deal of hope that future versions of InDesign CC will give us what we need to produce excellent ebooks without any need to do hand-coding. Almost all of our problems now are with the distributors and ereaders.

Now that Windows is the second-largest OS and will soon be the third largest—after Android and iOS—there may well be further changes. At this point, it does not appear likely that a tablet [iOS or Android] could handle an app like InDesign. But as the desktop computer fades into niche work, as MacOS blends into iOS, we do not know what the future will bring. I know several people who use InDesign on their Surface.

This book is current to the fall of 2016. But this is a rapidly changing industry. As usual, new information will be posted on *The Skilled Workman* and in other books until there is enough to do the next edition of this book.

ePUB & Kindle design in InDesign

I need to repeat the two basic assumptions before you can make an ePUB or Kindle book.

🐄 **First of all, you need the book completely written, edited, and proof read:** It's very painful to format a book that is not completed, unless you are actually writing in InDesign [which I recommend, as you know]. Plus, you certainly do not want a situation where you make changes in the ePUB which need to be added to the print version and so on and so forth.

🐄 **Secondly, you need to have the book completely formatted for print in InDesign:** This means that all copy is formatted with styles: paragraph, character, table, cell, and object styles. No local formatting is acceptable. If it is not completely formatted, you will have no way to control your ePUB globally and you will waste many hours and probably many days, weeks, or months.

Everything in HTML is formatted.

If you do not format it, your ePUB with be formatted with the HTML defaults—and they are horrible.

You have your book finished & formatted for print

Now, you are ready to start. Why do we start with print? Simply put: many of the quality extras you can use to help communicate with your readers are not available in Reflowable ePUBs and Kindle books [HTML / CSS]. This is especially true of your graphics. Though you can add color in any area you like, the resolution of your graphics will be very poor — 72 dpi in HTML compared to 2400 dpi for vector graphics, 300 dpi for continuous tone in print [Photoshop], or 150 dpi for ePUB FXL. From print you can start the process of dumbing things down to fit within the limitations of HTML, CSS, and ePUB2 or ePUB3 fairly easily. If you make a mistake or change your mind about anything, you need the high resolution, typographically excellent master from which you can start again.

Once you have that baseline, the modifications necessary for your ebooks become relatively easy—though never simple. At this point, for example, you need four versions for the font variations alone.

- **ePUB FXL [Fixed Layout]:** is a real good option for the iBookstore and Kobo.

- **Kindle Print replica:** This is their fixed layout kindle book built from the PDF of the book.

For reflowable ebooks,

- **EPUB Reflow:** Everyone now accepts ePUB2 with embedded fonts, with any font you have a license to use [through Draft2Digital], except for Kindle

- **KFX [Kindle Fire] MOBI:** you can try to embed fonts, but their formatting limitations with tables and lists suggest that a simple version with 4-font serif and sans serif font families is best. But all tables and lists need to be very simple, or converted to a graphic. As we will discuss at the end of this book, Kindle is still lagging far behind in typography and formatting. They have to do that to remain compatible with their older Kindles. It's the same problem the Windows OS has had historically. Plus, their Enhanced Typography strips everything out to use Bookerly.

With reflowable ebooks, the problem is that ugly, horrible typography has become the accepted standard. I find this vaguely nauseating, but I can no longer recommend going beyond the accepted—no embedded fonts, and worse for several of the suppliers.

Designing & formatting your ePUB & Kindle book without coding

With my assumption *[that you have a finished, formatted and uploaded book for print]* comes another equally important expectation. Writers and designers don't normally do well with code. It's not that we cannot understand it or use it. It's more like it is so boring and stifling to creativity that we simply avoid it whenever possible.

My experience is that creatives can handle a little simple Web coding like XHTML and CSS (actually, most of us have been forced into it for our Websites). However, most people who do what we do really dislike coding. It is a specialized skill not found often in creative people. Even HTML and CSS code writing is a painful process.

The question is how do we take these givens and produce an ePUB and a Kindle version of acceptable quality? It is not difficult, but you are certainly going to need to rethink your definition of book and of typographic excellence. This is a whole new world, with new rules and assumptions.

Do fancy ePUBs still require fancy coding?

At this point in the development of ebooks, ePUB design is commonly produced by coding specialists. That's no longer necessary. InDesign can export good validated ePUBs: FXL (fixed layout) and Reflow•able. Some things are still missing, but they're not just missing from InDesign but from all WYSIWYG applications. This was because of one simple issue. In order to do simple things like text wraps (CSS: alignments), sidebars (CSS: divs), and all the rest, before CC you had to crack the compressed ePUB file and mess with its innards (many files and folders).

CC has made major strides toward solving the text wrap and sidebar issues, plus they've solved many more problems. But, it is still not clean and simple. In addition, there are many design issues which suggest that text wraps and sidebars do not work well in ebooks, regardless. The largest issue is how to handle a div or text wrap which crosses a page break. If the reader changes the font or the size of the type, all the page breaks change also. **The ereaders have no real way to handle a graphic or a sidebar which crosses a page break.**

InDesign has become that simple program which allows you to do this visually—sorta. Anything more must be done on the code level and most of us are simply not ready to do that. It is possible to do the editing in Dreamweaver, but it is not pleasant and it is certainly not a good design experience. You are going to make some tough decisions about your ebooks. This is true no matter what you are using to format.

Bottom line: many things which are easily done in print and PDFs are impossible or difficult in ePUBs or Kindle

Here are InDesign's abilities
for the various versions

We will cover the details later in this book. However, I'm still including this here because so many people are trying to limp along with older versions. You really need the CC version.

InDesign CS5 and Earlier: have no real way to make ePUBs directly. Copy/paste into your HTML/CSS editor is your only real option.

InDesign CS5.5 can produce validated ePUBs: but your book layouts take a lot of work—and you'll almost certainly need to get into the code.

InDesign CS6 did quite a bit to write better code: but it still takes a lot of setup on your part. The ePUBs validate, but lists are compromised and embedded fonts do not work with the iBookstore. The Amazon plug-in for CS6 does better Kindle books than InDesign does ePUBs. But the plug-in cannot handle nested styles, for example.

InDesign CC is getting quite good at ePUBs

It validates and writes ePUBs with embedded fonts which upload fine through iTunes Producer or D2D. If you convert your lists to text upon export, lists work well. You can now add an index with active links. You can add a TOC anywhere with links to the anchors of the style in the TOC. This makes Lists for Graphics possible, for example.

Anchored object control now works—except for inline objects. They must be anchored as Above Line or Custom. They can now float left or right and it works with a text wrap. Plus the text wrap will let you inset your floating objects from the edge of the column. All of this works with iBooks. You do need to proof carefully though. It is not a perfect process. The conversion from PostScript for print to HTML for ebooks is rough. The difficulties may never be solved completely.

Most of these options supposedly work with Kindle KFX [but only if you own a Fire HD or better], But, in practice, you'll need to dumb down your KDP uploads substantially.

Draft2Digital accepts ePUB2 with fonts. Also you can sell DRM-free versions from your Website or through Gumroad or Ganxy. Increasing portions work in more and more ereaders. InDesign's ePUBs convert well with Amazon's free Kindle Previewer into KF8 books keeping everything until Amazon converts them again to enhanced typography after upload. A direct ePUB upload sometimes even keeps the embedded fonts in my Kindle apps for OSX and iOS. But Kindle remains very frustrating. Lately they have been reformatting the books after you upload into the new KFX format.

Even drop cap graphics like this can work with CC ePUBs: the major limitation left is that tall, narrow graphics get destroyed if the page break puts them partially on one page and partially on the next. I'm not sure what the solution is—other than using the break book before graphic setting. That often gives grotesque page breaks.

InDesign CC is finally a professional ePUB production tool: The largest advancement is the ability to produce Fixed Layout ePUBs. But, major advances have been made with reflowable ePUBs also. Tables now work fairly well with controls for stroke and fill—but no gradients yet. It is still very hard to get the width right also. A graphic will resize. Anchored graphics are now fairly predictable. The graphics now come in with the stroke and fill of the frame containing the graphic [probably without any gradients]. I don't know as I don't use this option. As with all ebooks, careful proofing is demanded. Not matter how skilled, you'll probably need several proofs. I do.

The ePUB limitations

Many of the excellent design possibilities of print are simply not available in ePUBs. What I intend to do is give you a list of changes you must make to get a validated ePUB that works. The good news is that several things that I would have had to mention 3-4 years are no longer necessary for CC.

Digital books are a very different world. You must rethink your concept of a book in order to design one which will work well for ePUBs and Kindle books. Let's talk about some of these necessary changes. But first:

Why are ebooks so different?

First let's talk about the fixed layout versions. These are very useful—especially if you are producing a book which will be used in a classroom setting. The fixed layout versions keep the page numbers, which are a real help in a group setting. There are three we use:

- 🐪 **Downloadable PDF:** This is a conversion from the print PDF using a color cover, color high resolution graphics and color in the text. I often do one in readers' spreads and one in single pages.

- 🐪 **Kindle's Textbook [print replica]:** This uses the downloadable PDF [single page]—converting it with the free Kindle Textbook Creator. I've been surprised at the good sales of these.

- 🐪 **The ePUB FXL:** This has some compromises: no justified copy and 150 dpi web graphics, but paragraph rules, fancy tables, and all the rest convert beautifully.

Yes, they may seem to only apply to non-fiction. But what about the study groups using your novel? A fixed layout version will keep them all on the same page [literally]. This can be important.

The Reflowable option

The most important factor is adjustable type: The reader controls font sizes globally and can override your font choices. At this point, even as a designer you get limited control over font choice, font style, font size, font spacing, or typography in general. But, the good news is that CC will export most of the CSS you request. The bad news is that the reader can still override a lot of it [and commonly will].

Plus, there are other issues: OpenType features are not available. CSS2 can handle this, but no ereader I know of is capable. We are back to the very limited 256 character ASCII choices. As a reader, in most cases, you get maybe two fonts with up to four styles, a dozen sizes (maybe), and that's it. Often you only get one font family—especially with e-Ink ereaders like the early Kindles, Nook, and Kobo.

As a designer, unless you embed fonts, you get the number of fonts available (just serif and sans serif at best, unless you're on an iPad), four typestyles (regular, italic, bold, & bold italic), largely unlimited sizes & line spacing, alignments, indents & paragraph spacing, nested styles (or hand-applied character styles), a couple of list styles, all set up with p and the six headline styles [h1-h6] plus unlimited classes, as a direct export from InDesign.

In most cases (except for e-ink Kindles, Nooks, and Kobos plus their apps on desktops, iPads, iPhones, and Android machines) you are able to control the serif and sans serif choices.

The second major factor is the single column layout: Liquid Layout with its automatic column additions and graphic resizing and mask changes for various ereaders and smart phones has no real bearing on ePUBs. It's developed for use in InDesign's Digital Publishing System [DPS]. That is, app design for magazines with tablets—where multi-column pages are the norm. And that is virtually dead from reader neglect.

We are not there with ePUB Reflowables: There is just not enough width to display two columns or more except for landscape tablets. Even with fixed layout ePUBs, multiple columns are rendered so small that they are virtually unreadable. However, non-facing-page landscape designs should work fine for FXL with a great deal of care.

 As usual, this is changing as you read this: Currently, it is recommended that you embed fonts for the iBookstore, ePUB2 uploads to Draft-2Digital, and DRM-free versions sold directly to readers using a resource like Gumroad. InDesign CC embeds fonts well. If I email a copy with fonts to my iPad and open it in most of the ereaders, it works well. The embedded fonts remain and the anchored objects render correctly. Kindle has issues, more on that later.

Even with Kindle, things change rapidly

As I write this, March of 2016, one major problem has been solved. With the release of El Capitan [OSX 10.11.3], Kindle Previewer quit working which made real trouble for Kindle conversion. Now, [yesterday, February 29] there is a new version of Kindle Previewer 3.0 [beta] which seems to work well.

Never forget, Kindle is in its own world with its own rules and proprietary procedures. Many of them remain outside our control. The conversion to better typography [the new KFX format] is done outside our control, without notice, and we cannot proof the results without buying our own version of the book. A 500# gorilla has few constraints. We just have to live with it [or get stomped].

The main problem is bad reader expectations

Any styling you put into your fonts, most of the uneducated readers will consider *wonky,* at best, and horribly ugly for the most part. But you cannot design for them. They will pick another font.

However, if you have embedded fonts, the serif/sans serif distinctions will remain. And they are the most important font information.

Ebook Design

Reflowable ebooks are like a different species. Of course, the basic difference is that you are reading on a screen instead of on paper. But it goes much further than that. There are many things which can be explained easily using typography in a printed book or even a fixed layout ebook. These can be quite difficult to accomplish in a reflowable e-book. Conversely, except for the e-Ink ereaders like the cheap Kindles, Nooks, and Kobos, all ebooks are available in full color—whether you decide to use their color or not.

So, we change how much? Everything.

It is obvious that we must rethink our book designs: The real question is how much do we want to change in the conversion from print to ebook? The unavoidable answer is that **we need a complete redo**. This goes quite a bit beyond simple repurposing. If you are going to use fixed layout ePUBs you may need two different redesigns: FXL and Reflowable.

Designing for quicker repurposing: This can certainly be done. What it requires is a clear idea of what is going to be needed for the conversion. In order to make your ePUB look as good as possible we need to think reasonably about how to set up our documents so they can be converted quickly. So, your decisions are very important when you set up your layout and formatting in your print books.

Everything must be controlled with styles

The major thing to understand is that HTML freaks out with paragraphs which use local formatting, done ad hoc in the document. All type must be controlled by paragraph styles, plus character styles as necessary. All graphics must be anchored and controlled with an object style. I haven't used the new table capabilities enough to have a definitive answer yet; but it is more than likely that table and cell styles are now necessary also.

The first e-book was the downloadable PDF in color

It's still recommended. There are places to sell them: Lulu, Gumroad, Ganxy, plus hundreds of others who specialize in free downloads and do not sell Books. You will be surprised at how many people will want a PDF to review, or simply to read. Scribd, Gumroad, Ganxy, and Lulu are the main ones we are concerned with because they will sell your PDFs.

Package your print version

So, all you have to do is package your completed book. This places a copy of your document into a new folder in an easy to find location of your choice. All of the linked graphics are copied to a new Links folder inside your new folder.

The production of your color PDF should be very easy if you have followed my suggestions about graphics. If so, you have a Originals folder which has all of the graphics used in your book in full color with the same name. You can simply copy this Originals folder into the new DownLoadable PDF version folder. If not, it can take quite a while to find the originals.

Remember, downloadable PDFs can use printing quality graphics & vectors

Then you can simply drag/drop the colored images into your Links folder. The grayscale images will be replaced by the color versions. Yes, you will have to make some image changes, but they should be minimal. Don't forget to use RGB as your color space.

There are a few other things you should do:

- **If your print book is normal, you will have a half title followed by a blank page before your title page:** You should delete both of those and replace your title page image with a full bleed, full-color cover.

- **Your Table of Contents:** It's an easy setup in the layout menu with the Table of Contents command to have live links and a complete set of bookmarks in the left column.

- **Other front matter:** should demonstrate a true benefit to the reader in the front. Or it needs to be moved to the back of the book.

- **Your index:** regenerate to have live links also.

- **Paragraph styles:** graphic portions of these like paragraph shading, paragraph rules, and so on should be converted from greyscale to color.

- **Publish Online:** you can use the Publish Online feature of InDesign CC to proof your downloadable PDF. If you are offering it free, Publish Online gives you a link to use immediately. This is a great new feature from Adobe. There's no way to use it to sell your PDFs, but it's a great way to offer your PDF in a universal format that works in all the major browsers. Your readers can be given the option to download the PDF, or you can just put it up there for reading online.

InDesign CC exports fixed layout: ePUB FXL!

I put the exclam on that because everyone is so excited about this ability. It is a big deal. It is essential for illustrated books like children's books. It's still not nearly as good as a PDF. **However,** the iBookstore will sell an ePUB FXL, and that's really good. Kobo Writing Life also accepts one. Neither will sell a PDF.

You start with your print version. The pages look very much like they do in a PDF. You can do headers and footers, page numbers, paragraph rules, and excellent tables. It even handles gradient paragraph rules and gradient strokes and fills on the tables.

Differences which might need correction:

- **They are still ePUBs:** with no OpenType feature support, no true small caps, and so on.

- **They also require Web graphics [150 dpi]:** like all HTML documents.

- **Some are pleasant surprises:** like the gradient strokes and fills within text blocks for rules & tables.

- **However, justified copy does not work**

I'll cover the rest of the rules for FXL as I go through the changes necessary for any ePUB export. Once you have it done, it's a simple export. The FXL option is easier to produce than the Reflow.

Ebook front matter

One of the first changes you should make for your readers is the elimination of as much front matter as possible. It is much harder to skip through such things in an ereader. This is also true with PDFs—even though they look very close to your printed version of the book—without spreads.

The good news is that you can put a hyperlink to where you want the reader to begin on all the front matter pages. Ebooks handle hyperlinks well.

Adding hyperlinks

One of the major differences with ebooks is the ability to use hyperlinks for your footnotes and references. The only problems will be companies like Apple, Amazon, Kobo, and Nook which do not allow links to competitors. Lulu does not allow links in ePUBs at all (though I haven't checked recently). Smashwords watches them closely. The rest of them only object if you have a link which goes to a competitor. Kobo doesn't like it if you have a book link to the Kindle store, for example.

Adding hyperlinks is very easy. You use the Hyperlinks panel. As you can see on the next page, you simply select what you want linked, open the New Hyperlink dialog, and paste in the URL. Or, in the case of the capture, type in the email address and add a subject line. You can easily add a character style for your linked text. If you do not, the default is usually a blue underline. I've tried special fonts and sizes, but that usually looks very contrived and artificial. The shortcut for a new Hyperlink, with the selected text or object, is Command+Shift+8. I commonly put simple button graphics on my master pages, with a hyperlink to a page—in this case the Table of Contents. This gives readers very easy book navigation.

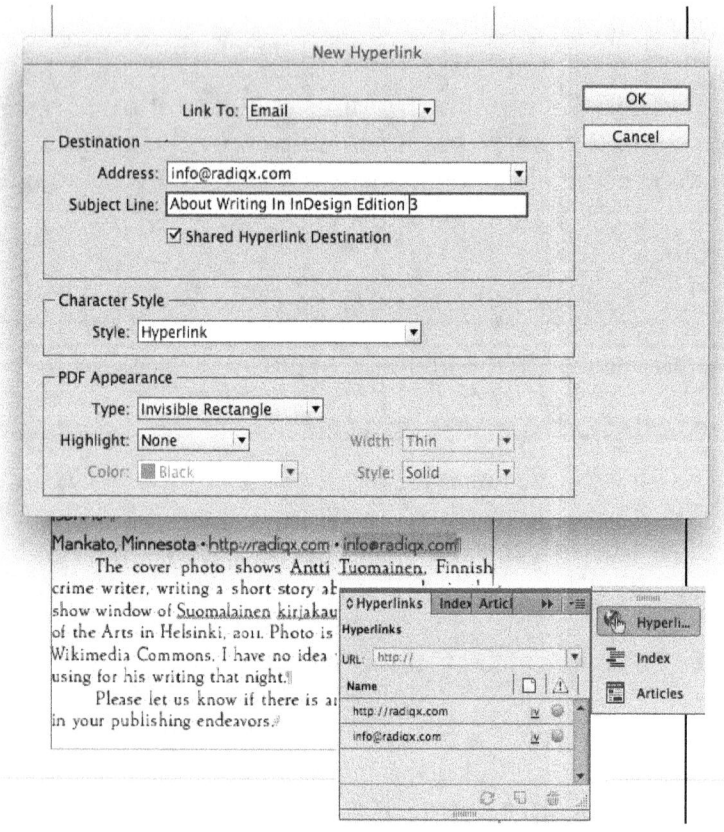

You can link to a URL, file, email, page, text anchor, or a shared destination. The hyperlinks panel itself will immediately show you if you have set up a functional link—and which type it is.

Contact info

It is very easy and necessary to add links to your email, FaceBook page, Pinterest, Twitter account, and so on. You want your readers to be able to get in touch with you. This is one of the strongest advantages we have over traditional publishers.

Many authors and publishing houses delegate all reader contacts to staff. That is not a good thing. The readers are looking for contact with the author or publisher. If you do end up with someone screening your email, make sure that personal requests are bounced directly to the author or person being sought out. This interaction with the readers is one of the great benefits of the new self-publishing paradigm.

 Apple will bounce your book for any links to Amazon, Nook, Kobo, and so on: They all seem to handle links to your own Website with no problems.

ePUB Design

With ePUBs we enter a whole new world. Normally this type of ebook is very fluid. Fonts and font size can easily be changed. Margins can be adjusted. Background colors can be stylized. The brightness can be adjusted to adapt to ambient conditions. You need to drop your preconceptions now!

To repeat again, I am assuming that you have a finished and formatted book for print and probably a downloadable PDF. The question is how do we take this and convert it to an ePUB ebook and a Kindle version? This question has become more complex now that we have the fixed layout option to export ePUB FXL books.

This field of design is changing so rapidly that anything a month old is at least a bit out of date. The good news is that the methods I will cover here will still work. The bad news is that some of them may no longer be necessary. After writing much of this material in the Spring of 2012, many changes happened during the rest of the year.

 In July 2012: the CS6 Kindle Export Plug-In was released. It was excellent and enabled embedded fonts.

 In the same month [7/2012]: Kobo began offering Kobo Writing Life so we could upload ePUBs directly into Kobo.

🐫 By the Fall of 2012: several other things had changed. Image sizing specs became available. A demand for ePUBs and Kindle Fire books with embedded fonts had begun to appear.

🐫 Now with CC: the instruction for lists has changed. The rules for CSS style tags called Export Tags by InDesign have changed.

🐫 April 10, 2013: Barnes & Noble dropped PubIt! In favor of a new site called Nook Press. It's had no affect on the tide rising against B&N, but no one knows.

🐫 The iBookstore no longer requires ISBNs.

🐫 InDesign CC now exports ePUB2s with embedded fonts which are acceptable to iTunes Producer, Draft2Digital, and Smashwords

🐫 CC 2014: began exporting ePUB FXL.

🐫 CC 2015: added Publish Online and Paragraph Shading.

These changes will continue. I remember that it took from the late 1980s until the very late 1990s before desktop publishing for print even started to settle down—and then InDesign changed everything. Now I can say with confidence that print production has not advanced much at all since CS2 or CS3. You can easily use old versions of software for print production.

This is not true for ePUBs and Kindle ebooks.

You need InDesign CC. The main problem is now ereader capabilities. This means you need to produce different versions: one with embedded fonts, one without, plus special versions for Kindle, possibly a fixed layout version, and so on.

They are all built within the same set of design issues. So, I want to take you through the options where changes will be required.

Document size

At present for ePUBs I am using a document with a Web intent: iPad vertical (768x1024 pixels), with 84 pixel margins right and left; and 112 pixel margins top and bottom. This gives me a Primary text frame of 600x800 which is nearly the maximum image size for an image in an ePUB on an iPad2. The Retina resolution (double the iPad2) has no standardized techniques yet. Nook and Kobo use the same width but shorter images [Nook 760 tall and Kobo 600 square?]. I'll cover Kindle later—but the Fire also likes 600x800 pages though 600 x 500 images are preferred and a 127K file size is better.

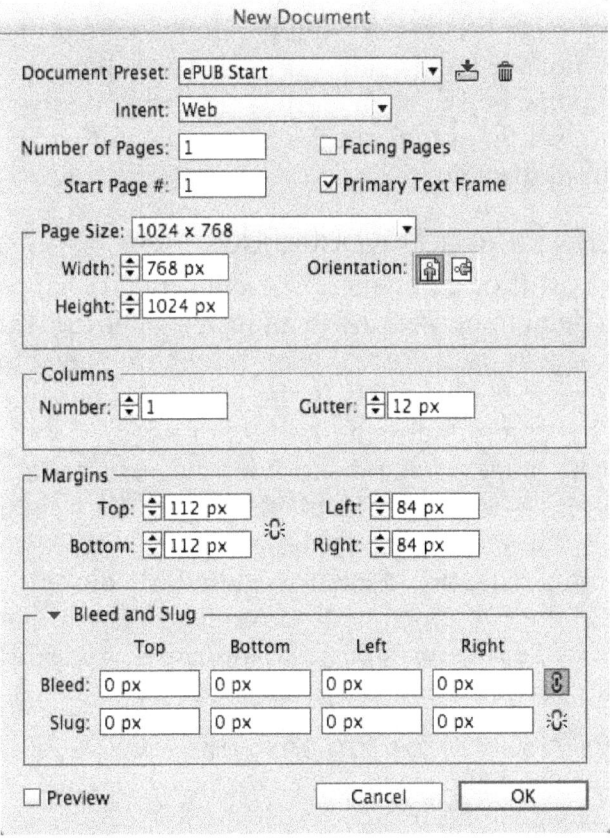

You just have a single master page because you cannot use page numbers, headers, or footers anyway [except in FXL]: Everything must be in a single story from the front page to the last word at the end. This is the old HTML page with infinite scrolling.

It ain't purdy, but it's what we have to deal with. And you can do a lot. Now that we have anchored objects which can reliably float left or right with a text wrap, things have gotten a lot better. The only real issue is floating graphics which cross page breaks. You need to watch this very carefully. In actual practice, floating graphics much taller than 100 pixels will cause problems sooner or later. The problem is that floating graphics which cross page breaks are simply eliminated and the readers do not see them at all. Normally you will want to make them attached to their own paragraph. Often you will need to set them to go to the next page (put a page break in front of them).

Page sizing for fixed layout ePUBs

This is still in its infancy. The conceptual change is that you need to be working in an InDesign document where the page is easily readable on screen. You need to make sure your body copy is in the 9-12 words per line standard. I recommend using half-letter up to 7" x 10". For landscape pages, I would shoot for the HD standard ratio: 960 pixels wide by 540 pixels tall. When I get a book which can use it well, I'll be using 9.6" x 5.4" as a starting point. That should easily handle two columns.

To use the FXL document to produce the PDF for Kindle's Print Replica versions, I would use 6"W x 9.6"H to keep the portrait book at the same ratio.

Just remember, limitations are the birthing place for creative solutions.

This is always the case. The first thing you do when designing a book is determine the limitations: page size, fonts used, and so on. It's always something.

Fixed layout ePUBs exported from InDesign can not display justified copy, as mentioned. This is due to what the InDesign engineers had to do to convert the page to a fixed layout. However, the solution they came up with now means you can use paragraph rules and gradients in an ePUB.

Graphic format, size, and resolution

This one is rough for those of us accustomed to print quality. Ereader graphics always look horrible when compared to print [except for the PDFs]. Even PDFs are stuck with screen resolution {though you can zoom into a vector graphic remarkably well]. What you need to understand is that you will be using relatively large Web graphics—but 72 dpi in most cases, not 300 dpi. This is obviously a serious conflict with the way we have been working for the past two and a half decades.

Basically you need JPEGs—a maximum of 600×800 pixel, RGB. For flat areas of color and sharp contrast, a GIF may look better. PNGs work also, but they are usually larger in file size. You just need to make your choices in Photoshop's Save For Web dialog box. The iBookstore, Nook, and Fire have different image size requirements as we'll see in a bit.

 Remember! Do not re-save JPEGs: Every time you recompress an image as a JPEG, you add artifacts on top of the other artifacts. Work in PSD with multi- ple layers or TIFF and save JPG, GIF, or PNG versions of the graphics for your ebooks with Save For Web.

This obviously takes some planning ahead as you will be using grayscale images (vector PDFs if possible) in your print documents—in most cases. You'll have CMYK images if you print in color. These bitmapped images will be PSDs preferably, and TIFFs upon occasion. So from the beginning, as you write and create, you need to save RGB versions of your color images. You probably also want color versions of your PDF graphics for easy conversions. Then using Save For Web as a Max quality JPEG [even High] will not noticeably ruin the image.

 Reflowable graphics MUST be to size and not cropped: Graphics must be placed at 100% and fit the frame proportionally without cropping. If not, your exported ePUBs will ignore the graphic. There can also be no corner effects, dropped shadows or anything like that. All these things work fine in FXL, but not at all in Reflowable.

At this point, even though the ePUB3 spec accepts SVG, which is a vector form of graphic, none of the ereaders do—with the possible exception of Kindle Fire and books produced with Apple's iBooks Author. InDesign cannot handle SVG images now, regardless. From what I have heard recently, SVG will work for what we need. Regardless, we need vector images for ebooks, and they aren't available. But there is hope. Use the Adobe Forums and start bugging them. They listen to the forums rigorously.

Everything in one story for reflowable

For reflowable ePUBs, you must remember the image of an eternally scrolling Web page. That is truly what we are dealing with. Of course, we want things like sidebars, inset text wraps, and so on. They work well in HTML. With certain limitations, InDesign CC can now export them. However:

The problem isn't with the ePUB standard

The problem is with the ereader hardware and apps available to read what we publish. I am always saddened when I read my ePUBs in iBooks on my iPad. They look so much better than is possible in Kindle, Kobo, or Nook. I know that purchasers of my ePUBs and Kindle books will be stuck with much less. An ePUB is a new capability [way less than a decade]. All I have to do is remember how limited PageMaker 4.2 and Quark 3 were when I began in digital publishing in 1991. Right now KF8/KFX on the Kindle Fire, Readium in Chrome for Android devices, and iBooks on the new iPad are best for type and graphics. Overall, iBooks is probably the best ereader available. But, I realize that many are still deeply tied to their e-Ink Kindles, Kobos, & Nooks. In fact, for many seniors, e-ink Kindle sales are still growing fairly rapidly now.

Eliminate all separate stories [reflowable]

Remember that everything in an ePUB must be in one story or in a div attached to it floating above line, right, or left. This is a radical conversion in many cases. And you will need to do much of it by hand. The Articles Panel is a help, but in my experience it takes longer to order things in this way and it is certainly not a flawless conversion. On the other hand, it's necessary if you add a linked index.

So, I drag'n'drop any separate stories into an inline location that makes sense—rewriting as necessary to keep the copy flowing well. Again, simply repurposing is not a good idea. ePUBs are a very different reading experience and we must adapt to it.

 The new paragraph shading option works well for sidebars: You can drop the sidebars inline in the primary Text Frame, then design the paragraphs with a shading in back to separate them from the regular copy.

What I find is concepts which can be easily shown with typography in a PDF are completely lost in an ePUB—even a fixed layout ePUB. I commonly need to rewrite copy to deal with this fact. Type in an anchored sidebar usually needs to be rewritten and placed into a different location to make sense as a part of the one story. Often, all text sidebars must be simply eliminated. Plus, OpenType features don't work.

 Live type in an anchored frame now works: BUT, you need to be very careful. The rewraps from point size changes often overfill the frames. The apparent type size is often larger. And in general, they simply do not look good. You can get borders and flat color backgrounds, but gradients haven't made it yet [except in FXL]. You can use a gradient in live type, sometimes [though it shouldn't work]. But, the stroke and fill of the frame are rasterized with the live type placed on top. In other words, the fancy frames are no longer resizable. Conversions to graphics work best in many cases.

Easily converted anchored graphics:

For very graphic books like mine with the wrapped graphics, I simply redo the object style for the graphics so that it drops them in Above Line or Custom locations. Moving graphics around to make the most sense becomes easy with the new drag'n'drop anchoring controls built into the frame edge—upper side, right corner. Simply drag them into position and convert them to the object style of your choice with a shortcut. I make many of my graphic conversions 600 pixels wide, because I want them as large as they can be to help you actually read them.

Wrapped graphics are definitely doable. They can float left or right and the indent can be controlled by the outside text wrap, which becomes the margin. The biggest missing capability is in setting sizing with percentages. Now, all you can do is set the pixel width. But the Tip icon in the next paragraph here is very problematic. I usually eliminate it or make a new 600 px wide version of some kind.

 Dealing with captions: Supposedly, they are grouped with the graphic and then set off with an Object style. I've had trouble getting the live text to work because it changes size with the rest of the text, and the graphic would need to be a grouped Object. That now works, but I don't trust it.

The Object Style controls

The new Export Options: in the Object Style dialog are pretty self-explanatory. You have three choices: Alignment & Spacing, Float Left, and Float Right. As you can see on the next page, you can control left, right, center alignment plus spacing before and after. The only strange thing is that Inline will not work for your Anchored Object Settings. It must be Above Line or Custom. If you leave it inline, no matter what it is, it will be re-rasterized and the result will be a mess.

Setting the text wrap will translate to the margins of the div inserted. So, I may need to adjust the text wrap a few times to get everything to line up as needed by my design. In a PDF, I commonly locally format these problems, but that does not work in ePUBs. You will need to make case by case adjustments.

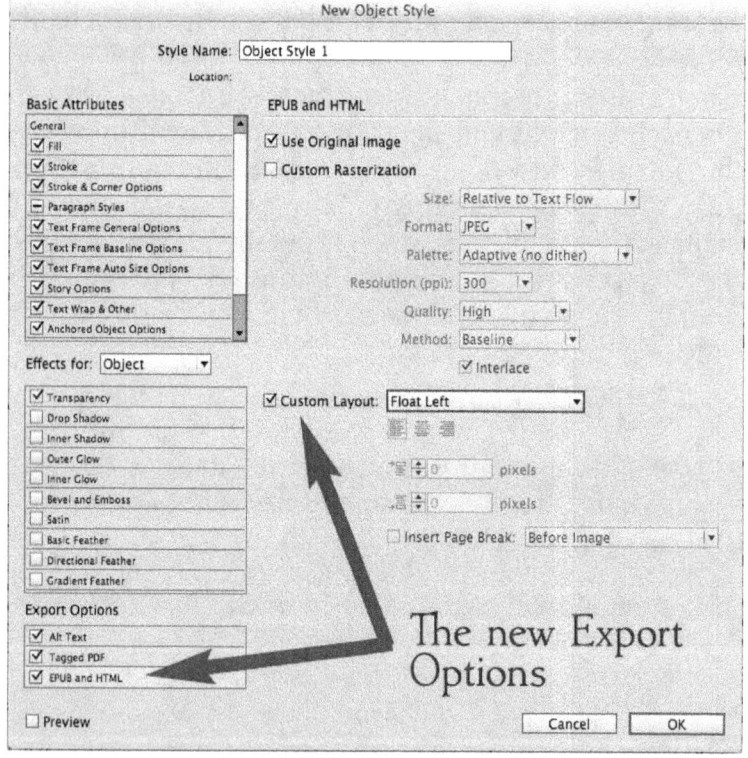

The new Export Options

Be patient with all of this: Adding ebooks to the publishing repertoire is a very complex operation for Adobe. InDesign CC 2014 was a major step upward toward a more stable, more usable, more easily exportable ePUB.

InDesign CC 2015 version added some more. We have been assured by Adobe that ePUB3 is very high on their priority list. *[In fact, I heard they joined Readium to add ePUB3 capabilities to ereaders.]*

Adobe has a good reputation of bringing these things online—and for doing it better than we expected. I know I certainly did not expect Liquid Layout, yet we got that for CS6. It may only apply to magazines at this point, but ePUB3 will probably use it more—both in InDesign and in ereaders. The iPad, Fire, and Kobo read simple ePUB3 docs now. Kobo promised full ePUB3 support by spring 2013. FXL works with their Kobo Writing Life. Now, as I mentioned, everything works quite well with ePUB2 Reflow, fonts embedded, and so on.

For CC 2014, I did not expect fixed layout ePUBs. As you know, what I am looking for is full CSS2 support. That's what we need typographically and it's basically available now. The fashionistas are demanding video and audio. The readers do not seem to care about that at all. They've got YouTube for that.

Fixing the styles

Eventually we are going to edit the exported tags. But for now I want to talk about how the styles need to change. The easiest way is to simply start editing the copy and changing the styles as we get to them. We must bear in mind that sidebars or anchored graphics require an object style with anchored object settings.

Again, often I find I need to rewrite copy in my books to deal with the reality of the ePUB reading experience. Do not hesitate to do that. However, my books are on formatting, so that's not surprising. Yours will not be, in most cases. So, little rewriting will be required. The main thing is to help the reader as much as possible.

Font changes

The big news, for me, with InDesign CC is that they can now embed fonts: These ePUBs are accepted by everyone except for e-ink ereaders. You have to encrypt the fonts to embed them. But the finished ePUBs upload fine through iTunes Connect, Kobo Writing Life, and Draft2Digital. Eventually, this will be commonplace and InDesign is leading the way.

Even though the ePUB spec says we can embed fonts, this is still spotty—not because it is difficult, but the ereader and reader support is commonly missing. Most readers have gotten so used to the ugliness of standard fonts and limited typography that they change your books to fit their expectations. That will radically mess up your typography. My current recommendation is still to embed fonts for iBooks, Nook, Kobo, Scribd, and so on. But you must make sure that you are using fonts with the proper licensing. You can also read embedded font ePUBs in BlueFire on the iPad and Readium in Chrome on Android.

Font producers like me can use their own, but you'll

Corinthian Light

ABCDEFGHIJKLMNOPQ
RSTUVWXYZ1234567890
abcdefghijklmnopqrstuvwxyz

Created by Letraset Type Director Colin Brignall, this clean-cut, monolineal sans serif typeface was inspired by Edward Johnston's Railway Type and Eric Gill's Gill Sans typefaces. *Myfonts*

Defining typography

- **Webster's:** The craft of composing type and printing from it; art and technique of printing with movable type.
- **Random House:** the art or process of printing with type; the work of setting and arranging types and of printing from them; the general character or appearance of printed matter
- **Cambridge:** the style, size and arrangement of the letters in a piece of printing
- **Wikipedia:** art of arranging letters on a page to be printed, usually for a combination of aesthetic and functional goals

What's unusual is ⟨Embedded fonts⟩ aries really get it. They ⟨Readium or⟩ but typography really has ⟨iBooks⟩ l act of arranging letters on

Obviously physical ⟩ onal shapes play a huge role in type design. But typography goes far beyond the actual shapes into cultural and

---

Corinthian Light

ABCDEFGHIJKLMNOPQ
RSTUVWXYZ1234567890
abcdefghijklmnopqrstuvwxyz

Created by Letraset Type Director Colin Brignall, this clean-cut, monolineal sans serif typeface was inspired by Edward Johnston's Railway Type and Eric Gill's Gill Sans typefaces. *Myfonts*

Defining typography

Webster's: The craft of composing type and printing from it; art and technique of printing with movable type.

Random House: the art or process of printing with type; the work of setting and arranging types and of printing from them; the general character or appearance of printed matter

Cambridge: the style, size and arrangement of the letters in a piece of printing

Wikipedia: art of arranging letters on a page to be printed, usually for a combination of aesthetic and functional goals

What's unusual is that none of the dictionaries really get it. They describe the physical act, but typography really has little to do with the physical act of arranging letters on paper for ⟨No fonts embedded⟩

Obviously physical considerati ⟨Kindle Mac App⟩ ole in type design. But typography g ⟩ the cultural and subjective responses

TypeKit gives CC owners plenty of good fonts to embed!

The main thing for us, in this book, is to have a little discussion about what will work and what will not for your ePUBs. Font choices are always a highly personal thing. I'm going to suggest my personal tastes and give you reasons. You make up your own mind. You can use the fonts I use in this book. I'll sell them to you cheap. Go to *The Skilled Workman* and look at the Fonts page to find some publishing font packages I am selling at very good pricing.

Verboten fonts [Courier]

First, I'm just going to mention the ugly ones you should never use: Courier or New Courier. These eight fonts should never be used unless you are trying to evoke a period, make a historical statement, or something strange. But almost everyone believes they are hideous fonts (not to mention they are very difficult to read due to the contorted lettershapes).

Fonts with bad reader reactions [TIMES & ARIAL]

These fonts are not bad designs, but they have issues—some of them fatal. I don't use them.

- **Arial:** This font family with dozens of styles is the cousin of Helvetica used to avoid the royalties. As far as I know, Microsoft had it designed precisely for that reason. These fonts plus Times make up the core of some of the most overused fonts in existence. Plus they are the default for many bureaucracies.

- **Times New Roman & Times:** These families normally have regular, italic, bold and bold italic. Though the bold pairs tend to be too narrow and ugly with plugged counters, the real problem is the bureaucratic associations. Times always brings up strong negative emotions for most people [except authors]. At best, it looks like a book designed in Word. This is why this tends to be the font family of choice for many authors. Just think "non-professional" to help with your cure.

Bureaucratic fonts: These are the fonts that have been the defaults in Office, Publisher, and similar non-professional page layout tools for decades—Arial, Times, and Times Roman. They are not very pretty fonts. The true situation is that non-professionals who use nothing but software defaults are the only people who use these fonts. In fact, most bureaucracies have standardized them and require their use. The only books to use them are those using Word conversions done by Kindle, D2D, and Smashwords.

Problem? Most self-pub authors are Word users: They tend to like Times and Arial because they are the fonts used as they write. It is yet another reason to write fully formatted in InDesign.

They trigger our bureaucratic drivel filter

For example, if you watch yourself when you open your mail or when you receive handouts, you will see that bureaucratic output is quickly consigned to the trash—usually without being read. Most people are fully aware that there is no usable content in these things. Bureaucratic output is produced purely to prove to administrators that something was done—even though we all know that nothing was done except some committee meetings. Our experience tells us these are a waste of time to read. Most of us throw them away unread (unless, of course, we are a member of the dratted committee).

So also, almost everyone simply tosses mail with obvious Word output without reading it—consigning it to the junk mail category in their mind automatically. Beyond that, default Word or Publisher output is barely readable. The default typography settings are very bad and obvious. There are simply too many really bad associations with these fonts to use them.

Versatile fonts for typography

The basic point is simple: You want to choose fonts that read well, have matching x-heights [if you use run-ins], and which will make the distinction between serif and sans serif in the CSS exported with the ePUB. These fonts are readily available *if* you have an ePUB license.

I want to mention some of the standards included in TypeKit. These come with an ebook license [https://helpx.adobe.com/typekit/using/font-licensing.html#sync-pdf]. There are font families that are relatively easy to read and comfortable for the reader. There are several fine serif choices, and many sans serif families. There are enough choices for you to be able to make your ePUBs unique, stylish and very readable.

For body copy you need at least regular, bold, and italic styles for your typographic needs. A bold italic is nice—but not often needed. You'll need these fonts installed on your machine to use them in InDesign. TypeKit allows you to embed and encrypt the ones which come with CC into your ePUBs.

I used to follow this paragraph with the complete listing of iOS fonts. But that no longer seems useful. The iBooks conundrum is one that I haven't quite figured out yet. It definitely does the best job of presenting your ePUBs with support for embedded fonts, floating divs, and anything that InDesign can export.

However, the iBookstore does not sell books I upload directly very well. Books uploaded through Smashwords and Draft2Digital sell much better through the iBookstore than the versions I upload directly through iTunes Connect and iTunes Producer. Now that D2D accepts ePUB2 Reflow with embedded fonts, the options have gotten much better. D2D distributes to iBooks, Nook, Kobo, Scribd, and more. At this point, the major lack is Amazon's poor quality book formatting.

So, what I want to do is simply suggest some font combinations that should work well for you. If you read my typography sections in other books where I commented on using a companion sans for your serif font, you'll recall that I said there that finding a good pair which works well together is difficult. I finally gave up and designed my own—the Contenu/Buddy pair until this year where I designed the Librum/LibrumSans combo I am using in this book. Both of these collections are for sale on my Website, *The Skilled Workman,* http://www.bergsland.org/hackberry-font-foundry/fonts/

Ebook standards are different

People who read ebooks are a new breed. Many of them are, like myself, shall we say, mature? A decent percentage of the new readers using ereaders are in their 50s or higher. We tend to like traditional typesetting, because that is what we are used to. However, even here there are some new trends we need to be aware of as designers.

In ebooks, I have seen several postings suggesting that non-fiction should be done with sans serif body copy. I would be very careful about that, but there is certainly no reason why you cannot choose a truly humanist sans like Optima or even Gill Sans for your body copy. Be sure that you pick one that is very readable. Then you can use elegant serif faces for your heads and get a beautiful book. I suspect that my next font design will be a readable sans to match with an elegant display serif. **Plus, the reader can change fonts at will:** Reflow is the goal. That trumps typography in an ebook. Also remember, that an ePUB on an iPad, or converted to KFX for the Fire, is the typographic wonder of the ebook world. All the other ereaders support ePUB. Plus there are many Android tablets with the Readium extension in Chrome. But without embedded fonts the font options remain abysmal. The various ereaders like iBooks, Kobo, Nook, and Readium all support embedded fonts. The Kindle Fire is certainly headed in that direction by supporting embedded fonts, but the Kindle apps often do not. So things are indeed getting better, but not entirely yet.

The Kindle, Nook, and Kobo choices may be easily readable on their e-ink devices. But they certainly do not provide good typographic choices for a designer. Your only real font choices might be serif or sans, plus you can add italic and bold. The bad news is that many of the ereaders simply ignore font instructions—but they might retain the serif/sans serif distinctions.

However, we must remember the ebooks using the currently limited choices are selling like crazy. Kindle still has a majority of the overall market, but the iBookstore is growing rapidly as the iPad becomes the dominant tablet for ereading. If you want to sell to that market, you need to make a book that fits their paradigm. In my case, non-fiction books about InDesign and font design sell about twice as much on Kindle as they do on iBooks (but print is still better than a third of sales). Nook and Kobo are still negligible (for me).

These percentages will continue to change regularly as the market matures. Since the Spring of 2013 I have seen radical changes in my sales. In the Spring of

2014, Createspace was still the biggest at 32%. Kindle was only 24% in the US but 32% globally. Gumroad had 12%, Lulu and Draft2Digital were both about 9%. Smashwords was a little less than 4% [it's mostly iBooks and Kobo]. The rest are negligible. In 2015, Createspace had about 30%, Kindle around 27%, and the rest were scattered all over. So far in 2016, Createspace is 38%, Kindle is 23%, Gumroad [sold from links on my Website/blog] is 13%, and the rest are scattered all over.

In other words, Amazon is barely 60% of my sales, with print nearly 40%. They seem to be slowly slipping. The domination of Amazon has run its course for me. I have heard others saying that Amazon's sales are going down. I suspect that will increase. Kobo is really making a push—as is the iBookstore. With iBooks is available in OSX, it should grow a lot. But everything is still controlled by the ebook distributors. One of these days that problem will be solved. At this point, I sell a lot through Gumroad links from my Website/blogs—as you see in the 2016 stats.

The problem is that most excellent text fonts for body copy have fairly small x-heights and there are not many sans serifs with x-heights that small. So, you will look long and hard for true companion fonts. The only font sets you are likely to have [in TypeKit] are Lapture/Calluna Sans, Sirba/Effra, or other large x-height combinations. Now you can see why I created Buddy and Librum Sans. Otherwise we're the victims of fashion.

❧ Contenu, Athelas, Garamond/Buddy
❧ Lapture/Calluna Sans
❧ Sirba/Effra

But enough on fonts. Let's get back to ePUB design possibilities. These options get better all the time.

Size & Leading changes

We have quite a bit of control here. In an ePUB the font sizing and spacing must be specified in ems or pixels. InDesign is doing it in ems. Basically, 12 point type is converted to one em. Leading is converted to a multiple of that em. On the iPad's high resolution screen, one em is actually 16 or 32 pixels high (32 pixels for the Retina). [But the reader can change it all by whim—though the size proportions you set will remain proportional.] **For fixed layout:** you may well need to increase your point size to get an appropriate number of words [9-12 words is necessary for good readability] per line.

Alignment

This was never a problem until 2014. But now **fixed layout, ePUB FXLs, cannot handle justified copy**. So, you must be sure to convert any style which justifies the copy. It's a small hassle, but it's a result of the coding process used. You just have to carefully proof your ePUBs and make adjustments.

Small Caps & ALL CAPS

Of course, because OpenType features do not work, true small caps are very rare in ePUBs or Kindle. So, any typographically excellent true small caps would have to be in fonts that have them like Copperplate & Bodoni 72 Small Caps. The OpenType variants will not be picked up. In the subhead before this paragraph, I am using small caps in the print and PDF versions. But I will set MALL and APS in a smaller point size [using a character style, but you will see they are much lighter] for my ePUBs and KF8 variants. Otherwise they would still not work in most ereaders. Even this workaround is commonly stripped out in the e-ink ereaders. **Note:** I've started making ebook versions of my fonts [Contenu eBook & Librum E]. Librum E has a special font for the small caps (Librum E Sm Cap).

No special fonts: CONVERT TO GRAPHIC

If you need a special font, you need to make it into a graphic [unless you can embed it]. For fixed layout, embedded fonts are the norm so this is not an issue. It would seem that selecting the words and choosing Create Outlines would do it. But the resulting rasterized graphic will be a bad size and very pixelated.

Normally, it is necessary to make a separate PDF graphic with that type so you can rasterize it into Photoshop. Then save as a PSD, then use Save For Web to make a Web graphic copy, and place that into your ePUB document. You will be doing this a lot—at least until the ereaders & distributors accept SVG or other vector files.

Remember: Embedded fonts have many legal issues. You need to be careful which fonts you use. Though you can embed any font you have on your computer in OTF or TTF formats—there are major problems. In many cases, you will need to pay extra for an ePUB license. So, if there is any doubt (and believe me there is), do not embed fonts unless you are sure you own the rights and that it will look good. You can go to the bergsland.org site and click on the page Hackberry Font Foundry for the fonts I am currently selling for ebook production.

But it is still very rare to buy a font which offers ePUB rights included. TypeKit is a good Resource. It is one of the real benefits of your CC subscription.

Lists

Lists do not translate well. HTML makes bad lists because of the lack of indent control—plus the limitations in the bullet characters available. For HTML lists, all you can do is delete all special indents you set up. Make it a numbered or bulleted list (with no special bullet) and let InDesign do the translation. It is not good. Remove all indents, left and right from lists unless you have InDesign CC. However, the numbering of HTML lists will not continue to separated paragraphs.

This problem is pretty much solved with embedded font ePUBs. It does quite well by using the "Convert To Text" option in the ePUB export dialog. For fixed layout, anything goes except for OpenType feature glyphs. Just remember, Kindle destroys lists using anything other than simple bullets. Plus, the lists converted to text option [it uses divs] totally freaks out the Kindle KDP conversion process when uploading. In KDP

Be very careful with fancy bullets: FROM LISTS

Prior to CC [specifically InDesign CC 9.2] this was a real problem. You had to crack the ePUB and change the CSS to use special bullets—from the limited CSS choices. BUT NOW, you can use any character in the basic ASCII set like the delta, lozenge, and so on. The problem is that in the basic fonts, those characters are not very good choices.

In my book production fonts, I have made bullets additions within the ASCII character set. This is one of the real lacks in TypeKit. Dingbat fonts don't really exist there—so finding a dingbat font with an ebook license is not easy to locate.

In CC, if you use convert list to text, this option embeds bullets with special fonts [including dingbats] when converting to text, but only out of the ASCII characters. The extra OpenType glyphs are not available. You can also make a Character Style with color and size changes to bulk up the bullets a wee bit. Beware though: Kindle KDP chews these options up badly.

All the fancy bullets must be stripped from your Kindle version, at present. Amazon wants you to use Bookerly, their font.

AaBbCcDdEeFfGgHhIiJjKkLlMm NnOoPpQqRrSsTtUuVvWwXxYy Zz 1234567890

Bookerly's a pretty font, as you can see—**very** *easy to read.*

Add chapter breaks with an H1 style

You must set up an H1 style (usually your headline) and specify it as the chapter break. Have it go to next page [not next odd page]. However, for iBooks, you can't do that either because it will add an extra blank page.

The good news is that even with your H1 style setup without the Next Page Keeps control, CC ePUBs still maintain the page controls and move H1 paragraph to the top of the next page.

Eliminate all soft returns.

A soft return is a forced line break in a paragraph without adding a new paragraph [Alt+Enter on PC or Shift+Return on a Mac]. You will get rid of all of them when exporting a reflowable ePUB. But understand, soft returns are a real problem when the reader can change fonts and font sizes at will while he or she is reading. If you must do a line break, you may well be stuck with special paragraph styles with no space between paragraphs to make it work. Soft returns seem to work fine with fixed layout ePUBs. Just make sure you proof your ePUBs carefully—FXL and Reflow.

Paragraph shading seems to work flawlessly

This new capability is quite nice. No, we do not have border control yet, but we can hope. I don't know yet whether the gradient will work in ePUB Reflow.

Eliminate all OpenType feature use

Nothing can be done about this. Current ebook readers do not support OpenType features. However, they probably will. It is part of the CSS2 scenario and therefore usable in the ePUB standard. This is a major change when moving from print and PDF to ePUB and Kindle books. Just simple things like Oldstyle numbers, 1234567890, require a special ASCII font to contain them. It's one of the main reason why I designed the Librum E font family for my new book production fonts. I'm using Librum in the print versions and Librum E in the ePUBs.

Eliminate tabular layouts

HTML/CSS does not support tabs so you'll need to do tables. The good news is that tables now work better, but not well. Kindle books still require converting tables to graphics with many of resolution/readability problems specified by KDP.

Use tables [FXL: good; reflowable: eh OK]

For reflowable ePUBs, you will often want to set up a separate InDesign doc for the table, export a print PDF, and rasterize that in Photoshop as wide as is possible [normally 600 pixels]. However in CC 2014, regional cell styles are supported as seen in the capture below.

Cell Styles			
Header Rows:	Headers	Left Column:	PartNumber
Footer Rows:	Footers	Right Column:	RowTotal
Body Rows:	PrintStrokes		

These choices are on the General page to the Table Style Dialog. CC 2014 also supports strokes, fills, and padding. Rules are limited to solid, dotted, and dashed. **A quirk:** A border color of [None} maps to [Black]. I am still regularly disappointed at how bad tables look in Kindle. In FXL, they work very well. In ePUB Reflow they are still a bit iffy.

Tables in Fixed Layout ePUBs

Here the problem is solved. So far, everything I've tried has worked flawlessly in my fixed layout ePUBs: gradient borders and fills, any rule style [wavy line, triple line, or anything], and basically anything you can do for a PDF you can do for a fixed layout ePUB.

Eliminate paragraph rules for reflowable

Fixed Layout ePUBs do paragraph rules well: You can do white or colored type over a gradient rule. You can even extend your rules outside the text frame. The only quibble I found was that these rules are cut off at the text frame border, *unless* there is also a graphic out in that sidebar area as you see on the next page. Then the paragraph rule is cut off even to the outside edge of the graphic. This is why I continue to say that you need to keep experimenting. You will find neat solutions.

For the reflowable ePUBs, the only rules you have available are Underline and Strikethrough: without any customizing allowed. If you need the rules, you can create graphics that you can place before and/or after your paragraphs. The only problem with that is the difficulty with spacing control. Plus there is no way to do an overlap so you cannot have a rule as a bar from which the type reverses out to white. On the other hand, we are able to use simple tables with color variations for the top and bottom borders. You just need to test and see what works.

InDesign's forte is graphic assembly

The whole procedure I just described took less than a minute—real time. Well, actually, two minutes because I was careful to set the type well. So, I was able to copy/paste a complex drawing into editable paths in InDesign in less than a minute. Obviously, getting editable pieces from Illustrator is quick and easy.

Using the brushstroke as a frame

To make a radical change, I modified the size of the circle to overlap the brushstroke, and pasted a picture of my home into the circle. This took another minute—with the result seen above. I added the type on top in another 20-30 seconds [the only glitch was that I had to set the new text frame to ignore text wraps as I had put a text wrap on the graphic automatically when I styled it with an object style]. Regardless, the whole thing was done

Paragraph Rule

A Minnesota winter at home!

in far less time than it took to write this explanation. It is dramatic if not too inspiring.

If I wanted a graphic I could use anywhere. All I would need to do is copy and paste the new graphic onto a new single page document, save it, and export it as a PDF [which I did]. If you are looking at this in an ebook, you can see it is in glorious 600 pixel-wide RGB color—rasterized in Photoshop and exported as a JPEG. For the B&W book, I could have rasterized into Photoshop and saved as a Grayscale PSD at 300 dpi.

You can do graphics like this very quickly. If you have the pieces at hand, any graphic of this nature can be done in less than a minute. Fancy tables with inserted photos and complex typography can be created in a separate document and exported as a PDF to be used wherever needed at whatever size you need.

Eliminate borders

You can use borders as a stroke on an object: But it depends on your version. For CC 2014, strokes almost work as expected, but only solid, dotted, and dashed. However, proof carefully. This one is still under development. There was nothing new for 2015, but one of these days we'll get complete border controls.

Tables will probably be the final solution: In CC, you are able to use single cell tables and their rules—sometimes.

Type color

You can make your type any color—but test. Gradients do not work in type color, but work everywhere else, for example. That's why the footers below [in the print, print replica, and FXL versions use a gradient for the rule, but a simple tint for the type.

CC now works with nested styles

You can use nested styles in your ePUBs. In the exported ePUB they are converted to spans which you can control with the Export Tags dialog. The only fly in the ointment was four-five years ago when the Kindle Export Plug-In did not support nested styles.

The Kindle plug-in did not handle nested styles for CS6 & earlier: It was a pain! I found myself just setting all the run-ins with special selections and character styles added by keyboard shortcut.

However, for CC I am going back to nested styles. I am making a special ePUB for Kindle [more on that in a bit] and then uploading the ePUBs directly in KDP. If you convert your KF8 books from an ePUB with Kindle Previewer 3 most of this information survives, depending on the day, week, month, or year. Kindle books are really frustrating. Sometimes you'll be sure you have it figured out and then the next day it won't work again. This is why I am going to be making the suggestions for Kindle in the last chapter of this book.

Pages & master pages

Reflowable ePUBs: these are irrelevant as there are no pages in a reflowable ePUB.

Fixed layout ePUBs: Because they do pages, master pages with automatic page numbers work well. The master page items shown below work fine. Actually, I had problems as the gradient paragraph rule worked, but I had to take the gradient out of the text itself.

Keep on experimenting!

 For example, this is a dropped cap graphic: It works fine in ePUB FXL. But, I have not found a solution to make it work consistently in a reflowable ePUB. At this point, for the reflowable versions, I will replace the dropped graphic with a Below Line graphic before the paragraph. It's not nearly as elegant, but it does work.

These compromises are normal in graphic design, if you've ever done any of that work. But, most authors have not. So, for the authors, experiment, ask questions, use your creativity. Just remember that the only thing that really matters is the readership.

Just be aware that your readers may be more sophisticated than the new authors are.

As an example, most people over 40 years of age will find most ePUBs and Kindle books look very cheap. Plus, they are very hard to read.

For millennials and younger, they will probably think things look fine, as they are used to the poor type of Word, the Web, and social media.

That's why I try to get an iBooks version if at all possible. EPUBs look the best there. But, many of the books are set with word processor sensibilities. This causes a negative reaction in me which is hard to ignore. It makes me think the author is young or new or unprofessional or worse. My wife refuses to even read them (and she's a voracious reader of romances).

Making these changes & proofing

What needs to be done now is to go through all the styles used in your print document and convert them to work within ePUB limitations. Then export your ePUB and open it in Readium [in Chrome] and in iBooks. For Nook & Kobo, I email the ePUB to my iPad and open it in the readers. ADE4 is making the other ereaders work better. BUT you need to proof on the ereader, it will show your fonts on the desktop computer because they are installed there. That will not happen in the ereaders. You can set the export options to automatically open your ePUB in your best ereading app after it is exported.

If you own an iPad, Nook, and/or Kobo: open the ePUB in it to see how it will look there. They all have procedures to sideload ePUBs. Email it to yourself and open it from the email into the reader(s) of your choice with the iPad. It is especially important to check out the graphics and see how they fit. Adjust spacing as well as you possibly can. Be very careful to look for issues which work well in print and PDFs, but do not translate well to HTML—like soft returns, paragraph spacing, OpenType feature use, and so on. Kindle proofing is always very iffy unless you own one. Even then they vary greatly from e-ink, to greyscale to Fire to Fire HD, and so on.

If you are typographically trained and visually sensitive, this first attempt at an ePUB will be a horrible shock

The typographic ugliness of HTML after you have so carefully crafted your typography in your printed book is a major hit to the senses. Your ebook readers will not be shocked. But, there is no kerning or tracking, and spacing is very crude. All of your OpenType features will be gone. All the controls are very crude—even with the new print quality screens. But most of the new phablets and tablets have 300+ dpi resolution for checking graphics.

Take a deep breath! Now get on with it!

You've learned to deal with this level of quality with Websites. *[If you haven't—shame on you!]* This is the reality of ePUB. Now your goal is to make it as easy to read as possible. It is likely that your first attempts will require you to fix several of your styles. Thankfully, they control the entire document globally because everything is formatted with no local formatting. This is why the use of styles for everything is so critical.

Deal with reality

Do not hang on to impossible design requirements. The more simple you make your typography, the better it will work in this greatly restricted environment. There is nothing wrong with ePUB and the ePUB standard. It is simply different and requires a new sense of design. As InDesign has improved we have more control. The largest hurdles at this point, and for the near future, are reader preconceptions and ereader capabilities.

ePUB does give us much more

If we quit looking at ePUBs from the background of the printed book and start looking from the background of ebooks, then we can see how much we have available in an ePUB. Just focus on readability. If your readers have to work at reading your book, they'll try changing the size—but more likely they'll just quit reading.

Setting chapter breaks

This is a very important part of setting up your styles. Reflowable ePUBs do not support page breaks—with one exception. If you have a style set up as a headline, with the keeps set up to start on the next page, the ePUB will start a new chapter when you use that paragraph style. But you must choose it when you export the ePUB. You find this choice in the ePUB Export Options dialog box: Break Document at Paragraph Style with a popup menu to pick the style.

 For iBooks: The set up just mentioned above does not work for books set up to upload to the iBookstore. For them you need to leave Keeps set to Anywhere, and then check the style to Break in the Export All Tags Dialog. This will give you the page break without an extra blank page.

Setting the TOC (THIS IS REQUIRED)

You do need to set up a TOC (Layout>> Table of Contents). You will chose this Table of Contents style in the ePUB Export dialog. The styles you choose for your TOC will be added to the bookmarks in the column to the left of your ePUB. You do not use leaders or page numbers, like you see in the print settings on the next page, as leaders do not work and page numbers do not exist in ebooks [more accurately the page numbers would change all time with reader changes to fonts and/ or type size]. ***Practicality rules in these things.*** You can spend a lot of time and money trying to figure out why these things are so or you can publish books.

Table of Contents		

TOC Style: [Print]

Title: [Contents]   Style: [7–Sub 1]

OK
Cancel
Save Style...
Fewer Options

Styles in Table of Contents

Include Paragraph Styles:
- 7–Sub 1
- 6–Head

Other Styles:
- [No Paragraph Style]
- Index Level 1
- Index Level 2
- Index Section Head
- [Basic Paragraph]
- 0–Alphabet

<< Add
Remove >>

Style: 6–Head

Entry Style: [TOC Heads]

Page Number: [After Entry]   Style: [Page#]

Between Entry and Number: [^t]   Style: [SmallLeader]

☐ Sort Entries in Alphabetical Order   Level: [1]

Options

☑ Create PDF Bookmarks   ☐ Run–in
☑ Replace Existing Table of Contents   ☐ Include Text on Hidden Layers
☑ Include Book Documents
☐ Make text anchor in source paragraph

Numbered Paragraphs: [Include Full Paragraph]

I publish.

Keep working on ideas. As you add a new technique that works, implement it. InDesign CC will continue to get better. But the basic concept is that you can only do what the software enables. A double-minded person will get nothing done.

Writing the metadata (THIS IS REQUIRED)

You need to write the metadata before you export the ePUB. However, you can enter the metadata within the export ePUB dialog box. As you can see on the next page, this is old File Info dialog box. The important things here are the title, description, keywords, and copyright. You worked all this out when you released your book for print. Right?

You find this dialog in the File menu under the File Info command. It is required to fill out this description page. It contains the information primarily used by the search engine spiders. So, obviously it will greatly help as your readers try to find a book like yours.

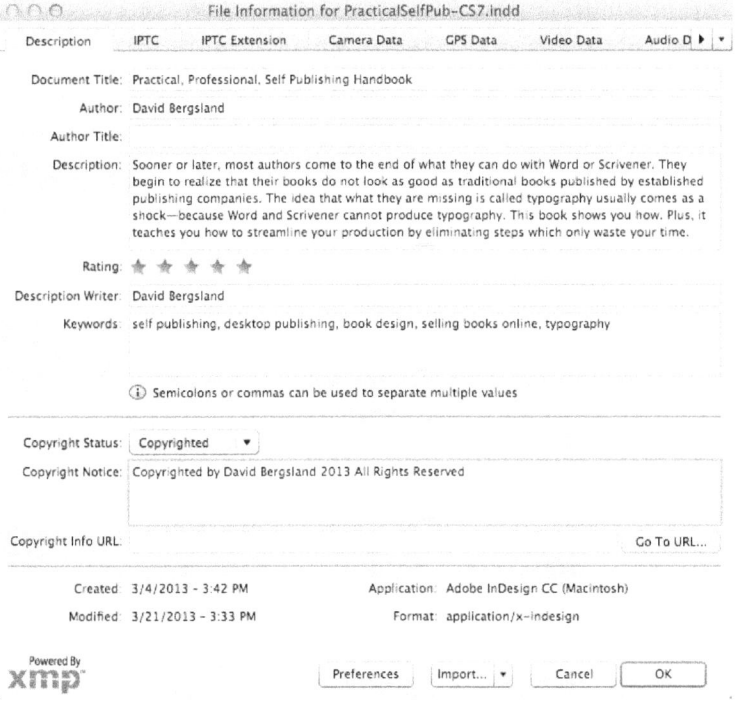

There are some strict rules for metadata

Some of these rules are Apple's rules. However, many of them seem to be Lulu and Smashwords paranoia. It doesn't matter. **Do what they ask.** You do want to sell your ePUBs, right? They include things like the metadata title must be identical to the copy found on the cover. It must be in title case except for a half dozen or so tiny words. There are several others things like this. For example, I had the title of an earlier edition as: *Writing In InDesign Second Edition*. Lulu made me change Second Edition to a subtitle. I was very irritated, but you can't fight city hall. Here are just a few from Lulu's page (these materials are six years old now. Get the latest versions on the Lulu Website).

Their list of rules is much longer: In fact, if they didn't sell so many books they would not be worth the effort.

- **Title must match everywhere:** metadata, cover, and book's title page

- **No mention of included materials that don't exist in the digital product:** (Example: CD, poster, etc.).

- **Cannot up-sell to a version of the product that is more complete.**

- **No advertisements or links:** in the metadata.

- **Do not use characters which require entity references in the description:** (Example: &, -, or –, curly quotes, etc.). This has gotten so bad with Kindle KDP, I normally copy/paste my description into an HTML editor, like Text Wrangler, to strip out all the bad characters. I find I must do this to get KDP to approve my descriptions.

- **Cannot mislead buyers or misrepresent the ebook:** (Example: An illustrated guide containing no illustrations or pictures).

- **Do not use font sizes in the description:** Not HTML at all. For KDP, you can fix that once the book is listed on your author page. The description editor has several options.

☞ **Subtitles are particularly important for differentiating multiple books:** in a series that share the same title.

☞ **Improperly formatted HTML tags in the description:** can cause a garbled description in retail channels.

☞ **Titles and Subtitles incorrectly capitalized. The first letter of all words in the title and subtitle should be capitalized, except for the following words:** a, an, and, for, from, of, or, the, to. The first and last word of the title and subtitle should always be capitalized.

☞ **Use of HTML lists in description is forbidden**

☞ **Titles beginning with articles should display properly. EX:** A Tale of Two Cities, not Tale of Two Cities, A

☞ **Must have a valid description:** Do not use the title.

☞ **Multiple blank pages:** Especially at the beginning of the book. Please remember to remove blank pages before converting to ePUB

If you do not follow all of them precisely, they will not publish your book. I signed up with Apple Connect so I could upload my ePUBs directly. I think you can see why—I simply do not need the hassle. However, books sold through Lulu, Smashwords, and Draft2Digital continue to sell much better than the versions uploaded directly. Draft2Digital does not require much of this nonsense—so it's my distributor of choice now.

There's been a big change, starting in 2015: I started using ePUB2 Reflows with embedded fonts uploaded to Draft2Digital for iBook, Nook, Kobo, Scribd, and several others. Most of the metadata rules seem to be relaxed [a little]. Plus, we now fill out the metadata in the ePUB export dialog. In 2016, I commonly publish in Createspace, KDP, and D2D. I also put an archive up DRM-free on Gumroad.

Setting the Export Tags

As mentioned, this ability to open a single dialog box and set all the HTML tags and add the CSS classes for each style is huge: It is a real disappointment that we cannot edit these class rules directly, but it makes it much easier to edit the CSS—if you're into that type of thing. CC works well, but it has added a couple of wrinkles. Nothing major.

You can easily force InDesign to write good CSS

Well, that's a bit of an overstatement. The Web developer purists will be shrieking. But, you can easily make InDesign write CSS that controls all of your type in the ePUB in most cases.

Lists

The only exception is lists. HTML lists are ugly and hard to control regardless—even if you coding directly into a Website, but CC has a solution for this problem also. With CC, it turns out that setting the ePUBs conversion for lists to [Automatic} works for Kindle. For everyone else, the standard HTML lists will never work typographically. In the Export to ePUB dialog, Convert To Text works best. I change from [Automatic] to p:bullet or p:number for the tag and class. This comes closer to retaining the indents and the special bullets. CC does retain custom bullets from dingbat fonts. But this does require embedded fonts.

The good news is that cracking the ePUB and editing the CSS is no longer necessary: You can easily force InDesign to write CSS rules that will control all of your type without the need to edit the CSS afterward. What you need to do is make sure that you specify a class for all your styles as well as a tag. The first thing I do is choose the Select All Unused command and delete all unused styles that were selected [except for styles which will be used for the TOC].

Let's look at what I exported for an ePUB with a recent book. I opened the Edit All Export Tags... dialog and set up the tags and Classes. You can see them below. The only difference now is that I uncheck [Basic Paragraph], [Basic Graphics Frame], & [Basic Text Frame].

Edit All Export Tag

Show: ⦿ EPUB and HTML ○ PDF   OK

Style	Tag	Class	Split EPUB	Emit CSS
¶ [Basic Paragraph]	[Automatic]		☐	☑
¶ 2–body	p	norm	☐	☑
¶ 2–No first	p	nofirst	☐	☑
¶ 2–run-in	p	runin	☐	☑
¶ 3–Bulleted	p	bullet	☐	☑
¶ 3–Description	p	nnobullet	☐	☑
¶ 4–Body heads	h3	small	☐	☑
¶ 5–Tips	p	tip	☐	☑
¶ 6–Head	h1	normh1	☑	☑
¶ 7–Sub	h2	normh2	☐	☑
¶ 8–9(WavyRule)	h2	italic	☐	☑
¶ 8–Sub	h3	normh3	☐	☑
¶ TOC Heads	h1	indexhead	☐	☑
¶ TOC Sub1	h4	indexsub	☐	☑
A 1–bodyBOLD	strong	body		☑
A 1–List Bold	strong	sans		☑
A 2–Italic	em	bodyitalic		☑
A 3–BoldItalic	span	smash		☑
A 3–ListRegular	span	sansreg		☑
A 4–Version	span	smallsans		☑
A Bullet	span	red		☑
A 14 point	span	fourteen		☑
⊡ [Basic Graphics Frame]	[Automatic]			☑
⊡ [Basic Text Frame]	[Automatic]			☑
⊡ 3–Inline	[Automatic]	three		☑
⊡ 4–Anchored	[Automatic]	four		☑
⊡ 5–SimpleAnchor	[Automatic]	five		☑
⊡ 6–Left	[Automatic]	six		☑

Cancel

Notice I added tags for all the styles. I do not leave any set to [Automatic] except for the Object Styles. The CC difference is this: if you do not use unique classes for every style InDesign will scream bloody murder with alerts. I tended to do it like I do with my websites, using the same class for all items in a div. But for an ePUB, this does not work. So instead of classes like: p.norm; and h1.norm, I have to use something like p.norm, and h1.normh1. It's a minor irritant and it does solve the problems. The CSS exports flawlessly [at least for everything other than Kindle].

I must decide whether the paragraph style is a subset of p, h1-h6. For character styles, I need to decide if the style is a subset of em, strong, or span. This will work, and it will look remarkably close to what I see in InDesign. I'm no longer editing the CSS in Dreamweaver. In fact, I was so sick of it I quit a little early with CS6. CC improved things. With CC2014 things were better. CC2015 was even better. CCnext will do the same.

Why add the classes?

That's simple. InDesign would not define p, my basic paragraph tag. But it will define p.norm. It will not define h2, but it will define h2.normh2. Is the result wonderfully sleek and elegant XHTML code? No. But it works and all of your typography is controlled. If you do not do this, you are forced to crack the ePUB, open template.css, and add the basic tags. So, the choice is yours.

You can now design your ePUB edition of your book in InDesign and directly upload the resultant ePUB with no modifications. The results will look very good. Purists might tear their hair, but I think it's silly to add coding which does not help much—especially with ereaders being so bad.

The reports are that for ePUB FXL the code is better than most hand-written code.

the top listings are many fonts I don't want to use in my ePUB, because every ereader would substitute them out into its defaults unless they were embedded [and for some I do not have an ePUB license]. I am using 130 fonts so far. Obviously this is real problem with an ereader like the Nook which only has three fonts available. More importantly, you must be sure it is legal for you to use them. None of these 130 fonts are available on any ereader unless I embed the fonts.

I will use this dialog extensively to check the ePUB version of this book. I must eliminate any font for which I have no license. Plus, I do it simply to control the file size of the ePUB which is already huge, I must convert all of these fonts to graphics. I will carefully decide what to do with each one of those instances where a font is used—deciding how to convert it to a graphic you can read easily.

 This may add many graphics to your ebooks: If you have books like mine which are written about book design, you have some unique problems. I had to make many new graphics to show simple things I could easily demonstrate in print like ligatures, small caps, oldstyle figures, small cap figures, ordinals, ornaments, and so on.

If I click the More Info button you can see in the Find Font dialog, it will show me the page location of the font use. Once I locate the font flagged in the actual copy of the book, I find I have one of three issues to deal with:

- **It may be in a paragraph or character style that was never redefined:** In that case I can redefine the style and globally eliminate the font usage very easily.

- **It may be in a graphic:** In this case I must make a rasterized version of the graphic. Live

The goal is an easily readable book—not the pro-duction of a coded tour de force. You need to closely examine the output for readability.
That's your priority.

It is never quite that easy: bad fonts

The problem is that during the massive conversion from your print version to your ePUB version it is likely that you have many styles or locally formatted type that use fonts you cannot use in an ePUB. A couple of years ago, I was looking at the CSS for the first proof of the ePUBs and at the bottom I found many spans asking for fonts I was certain I was not using. They had been added along with old copy.

We See, above, the Find Font dialog box (Type>> Find Font...) for one of these books. As you can see, type in a graphic will normally cause too many problems in the display of the type to be used. Sidebars with live type are always going to be a very tricky thing in an ePUB.

🐄 **It may be part of the copy:** This will probably not happen to you unless you are like me and write about typography and fonts. In this case, you can select the type and Create Outlines—leaving the outlines type inline in the copy. That will work, but InDesign will convert that outlined type into a coarse bitmap that looks pretty chewed up. Your best choice (for quality) is to rasterize that type in Photoshop and save it as a high quality JPEG at 72 dpi, 600 pixels wide. You can then place that high resolution bitmap graphic as an anchored object in your copy and it will look as good as possible.

Once you have your fonts cleaned up and your export tags set, you should always recheck your TOC settings and your File Info. Then you can export your ePUB. Type Command+E and select ePUB for your format.

EPUB Export dialogs: fixed layout, reflowable, 2 & 3

With InDesign CC, the ePUB export dialog gives us a lot of tools and options as we fought to control our output. There are six pages and many things you need to set for ePUB 2.0.1, and ePUB 3.0. Now we have two separate export dialogs for FXL and Reflow.

At this point, ePUB2 with embedded fonts works well for Draft2Digital: iBooks, Nook, Kobo, Scribd, and a few others. ITunes Connect and Kobo Writing Life accept FXL ePUBs. The ePUB3 support for reflowable is minimal. This entire area is changing, seemingly by the week, so any updates will be mentioned in my blogs.

The Fixed Layout ePUB export box

This is all ePUB3. In many ways, this option simplifies things a great deal. Fonts are always embedded, for example. The CSS is always written. This entire export process is fairly controlled.

The general page
Export Range: This gives us the normal choices.
Cover: The choices are None, Rasterize First Page and Choose Image. IMHO: you always want Choose Image. Just pick one that matches the page size. Once you choose an image that changes to From Location, as you see below. I design a specific front cover to be used and link it here. It should be the page size and 150 dpi. Just remember to use a JPEG optimized with Photoshop's Save For Web dialog for the cover, at this point.

Navigation: TOC Style: You need to choose the one you have set up for your ePUBs. As you can see I call mine ePUB.

Options: Spread Control. This is very different from anything we've had before. The choices are:

☞ Based on Document Setup:

☞ Convert Spread to Landscape page: Portrait books with facing pages and converted to landscape spreads

☞ Enable Synthetic spreads: Portrait books non-facing can allow synthetic spreads if the ereader supports it.

☞ Disable Spreads: Obvious

Conversion settings

Format: This has four normal choices: Automatic, JPEG, GIF, and PNG—no SVG yet.

Resolution: This also has four choices: 72, 96, 150, or 300 dpi. I've been using 150 dpi as I have tested this out. It seems to work well. The lower resolutions, not so much. **JPEG Options:** I've been using Progressive, and High as you can see. In my current workflow, I only use JPEGs. But for transparency, I go to PNGs.

GIF Options: I don't usually use these, but adaptive (no dither) is probably the best.

The real problem

I do not want InDesign to be messing up my graphics. Reconversions always blur the image, at least slightly. So, I'm doing everything I can to avoid that issue. It's not easy and often it just doesn't work. As I get clearer info from Adobe, I'll edit this and post about it in *The Skilled Workman.*

CSS & Javascript

I'm skipping over these. They simply have an attachment button to add your own CSS files or javascripts.

Metadata

This is a major change for CC 2014. From now on we will be filling out our metadata in the Export ePUB dialog box. If you already have the File Info metadata dialog filled out—and that is certainly possible if you are making a conversion from your print PDF to a fixed layout ePUB—InDesign will populate this page from the first page of the File Info dialog. As you all should know by now, this is extremely important information. It is often the major way readers find your ePUBs.

The keywords and description need to be chosen carefully and written well. Both of these areas are as crucial as your cover and title. Spend a lot of thought and prayer over all four of these items. If your books are not selling well, see what your competition is doing here.

Viewing Apps

This is the expansion of the old View ePUB after export checkbox. Now you can list the ereaders you have on your computer and view your new ePUB in all of them for proofing.

One of the things you'll need to do is keep on top of the new ereaders as they come out. Do not be surprised if you export and check out your ePUB, that you need to edit and reexport—often several times. I still have to do this, and I've been doing it a long time.

Reflowable ePUB dialog box

This covers 2.0.1 as well as 3.0. As mentioned ePUB2 is still needed for the distributors who will not accept ePUB3 like: Lulu, Smashwords, Tomely, NookPress, and the rest. These suppliers will not accept embedded fonts either. Why do we bother with them? They sell a lot of books. Draft2Digital uses ePUB2 to add a lot of helpful marketing to your books, like adding New Releases at the back of all your books, adding a list of your other books and so on. They cannot do this with ePUB3.

General

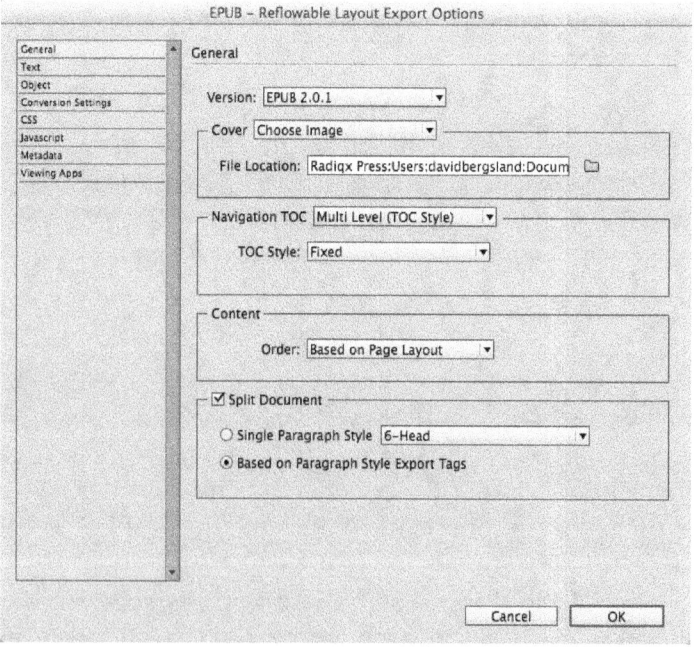

Version: the choices are 2.0.1 or 3.0. You will probably need two versions of this: a 2.0.1 with fonts and one without fonts designed to work a good as possible within the Kindle universe.

Cover: The choices are None, Rasterize First Page and Choose Image. IMHO: you always want Choose Image. Just pick one that is 600 x 800 pixels x 72 dpi. Use Photoshop's Save For Web dialog. That's what they all want. I design a specific front cover to be used and link it here.

Navigation: TOC Style: You need to choose the one you have set up for your ePUBs. As you can see I call mine ePUB.

Content: Based on Page Layout, Same As XML Structure, and Same As Articles Panel. I find the Articles panel useless for dealing with sidebars and the like. The only thing it works for is the TOC and Index, but those are added correctly by the page layout.

Split document: You can check the first option and pick the one paragraph style you use for starting new chapters. Or you can check Based On Paragraph Style Export Tags. In most cases, you want the second one as iBooks uses that whether or not you have the first button checked.

Text

Options

Remove Forced Line Breaks: That's what they are calling soft returns. You must remove them because the type re-wraps horribly when the readers change the size and font (and they will). When InDesign removes these soft returns it replaces them with a space. That is almost always what you want. But check and make sure.

Footnote placement: At the end of the paragraph seems to be the best method for readability of footnotes in an ereader—at least until the pop-up footnotes are accepted by everyone. IBooks takes you to the footnote with a link back to where you were. Most footnotes these days are hyperlinks—where you might actually hope that readers stopped the reading to go and read the source. The pop-up footnotes may well be the best. My clumsy fingers make the pop-up variety untenable.

Lists

Bullets & Numbers: As mentioned, HTML lists are very ugly. With CC, the best option is Convert To Text. It's not perfect, but the bullets are maintained and any applied character style, plus this comes the closest to the indents you set up in InDesign. But remember, bullets which are dependent upon a font will need that font embedded—I'll talk later about Kindle's distortion of lists.

Object

This is all puzzling. But for most cases, what you see on the next page works best. Fixed CSS Size only seems to work with iBooks. The basic concept is simple: now that it is possible to specify your original image—the one you carefully prepare in Photoshop—you are a fool to do anything else. You check Use Existing Image for Graphic Objects. You really do not want any software automatically doing anything to your images when they are so severely limited by the format. Web images, 72 dpi, are extremely crude. Virtually all detail is lost. For CC2015, images in ePUB3 are broken. They become very distorted upon export. It's another reason to stick with ePUB2 for now.

Finding out information on images is like trying to pull hens' teeth (and no, city folk, they don't have teeth). No one seems to want to admit how bad the images really are. The best I can find is that the iPad, most smart phones, and high-resolution tablets require 600x800 pixels or less. However, Kindle is now saying that we should save our images at 300 dpi JPEGs and PNGs. I'm going to be experimenting with this. But the file size of the book could easily get very large extremely fast.

☛ The iPad maximum is 600x860 pixels.

☛ Nook's maximum size is 600x730 pixels.

☛ For Kobo and Fire it is 600x800.

At this point, I make my images to size, and JPEG [in almost all cases]. I make them wide enough to fit the column of type and place them as Anchored Objects. With Kindle's new recommendations, I'm going to experiment with 300dpi images Saved As, instead of Save For Web. The problem is that I use so many and most of them are usually screen captures, which originate as low-resolution images.

With CC's new capabilities, I can use smaller images more easily. But tall narrow images will always be a problem. I try to do something to make the images wider so I can use the Above Line style if the image is tall. I do this to get as much help as I can with image sharpness. You can make them smaller and have them work OK. But, if you need detail make them as large as possible, and that is 600 wide portrait, and 800 wide landscape.

Remember, ebook graphics are ghastly: I continue to fight the good fight, but you really need to question why you are even including graphics. The iPad does a good job, but the ePUB format itself does not support graphic excellence. Of course there was the hope that the high resolution of the tablets would really help. But the file size is usually too large to use.

Preserve Appearance from Layout: I was very pleased with the Use Existing Image for Graphic Objects button. But Adobe Digital Editions 4 [ADE4] can't handle it. My procedure is to open all the graphics from the print version in Photoshop and make them exactly the pixel dimension I need. Then I use Save For Web... to save them as JPEGs. This gives the best results.

For print, I use PSDs (Photoshop's native format) at 300 dpi. I keep the original PSDs in case I want to go back to the way the image was before the JPEG compression. Then I save JPEG versions at 600 pixels wide [or whatever I need] to use in the ePUB. I should be able double the size for iPads with Retina Displays (and the higher resolution Android tablets), but it adds so much to the file size I haven't bothered yet.

Use Existing Image for Graphic Objects: Though this is what I want, ADE4 won't allow it.

CSS size: The choices are Fixed and Relative to Page. I use Fixed because of ADE4, but again this is controlled by the controls in the object style. I want them as large as possible to be readable because they are basically low-res bitmap images. Fixed works well with iBooks and ADE4. It's the only setting that works [this week]

Image Alignment and Spacing: Because my images are all anchored objects, the alignment is controlled by the object style used. But I set this Flush left.

Insert page break: Before Image, After Image, or Both Before and After Image. I rarely use it, but its utility is clear. Remember that page breaks destroy images. So, putting a page break before the image gives the best hope of an unbroken image. The extra page breaks really mess up your pages though.

Ignore Object Export Settings: I leave it unchecked because I do not set custom settings for any image. The problem was that Object Export Settings were needed to control anchored objects as sidebars. In CS6 and earlier, these settings really didn't work. Now they are not necessary.

Conversion

Format: You have four options: Automatic, JPEG, GIF, and PNG. I use JPEGs almost exclusively. With Automatic on, InDesign converts anything it can't use [like a PDF] to a PNG.

Resolution (ppi): I make my large images 600 pixels wide and 72 dpi JPEGs. I've been using 150 dpi for books with fewer graphics. For a book like this one with nearly 50 graphics, I go with 72 dpi to better handle the size of the resulting ePUB.

JPEG Options: I set the JPEG options to Progressive, High. The image quality in ePUBs is bad enough without any JPEG artifacts produced by compressing the JPEGs too far. However, for my font design book (with nearly 300 graphics) this made my ePUB nearly 20 MB. But then the ePUB for the full InDesign book is 22.3 MB.

This book is only using 50 images or so. As a result, the ePUB for this book will be much smaller. With the larger books, I am sometimes forced to change the quality to medium. Because the images are almost all screen captures, the new ePUB looks very good on the iPad. I may have to do that for this book also. You must do what you need to do to get the best images possible. **GIF Options:** I use Adaptive (no dither). But then, if I make my GIFs with Photoshop's Save for Web, I'll use 100% dither and a bit of lossy compression.

PNG Options: I take what I get.

CSS

Generate CSS: Unlike fixed layout, where CSS is not optional, it is in reflowable. I can't really think of a reason why you would not want to generate CSS—except for the obvious one: your own CSS is better and you want to use it.

Page Margins: Try it, but most ereaders ignore these.

Preserve Local Overrides: I uncheck this. You usually do not want any local overrides. Clean them up while proofing. They are covered with your character styles.

Include embeddable Fonts: This works for everyone now, with the functional exception of Kindle. If you are uploading directly into NookPress, they may not be accepted. I'm sure Lulu does not yet.

Javascript

I'm skipping over this. It simply has an attachment button to add your own javascripts.

Metadata

This was a major change for CC 2014. From now on we will be filling out our metadata in the Export ePUB dialog box. If you already have the File Info metadata dialog filled out—and that is certainly possible if you are making a conversion from your print PDF to a fixed layout ePUB—InDesign will populate this page from the first page of the File Info dialog. As you all should know by now, this is extremely important information. It is often the major way readers find your ePUBs.

Viewing Apps

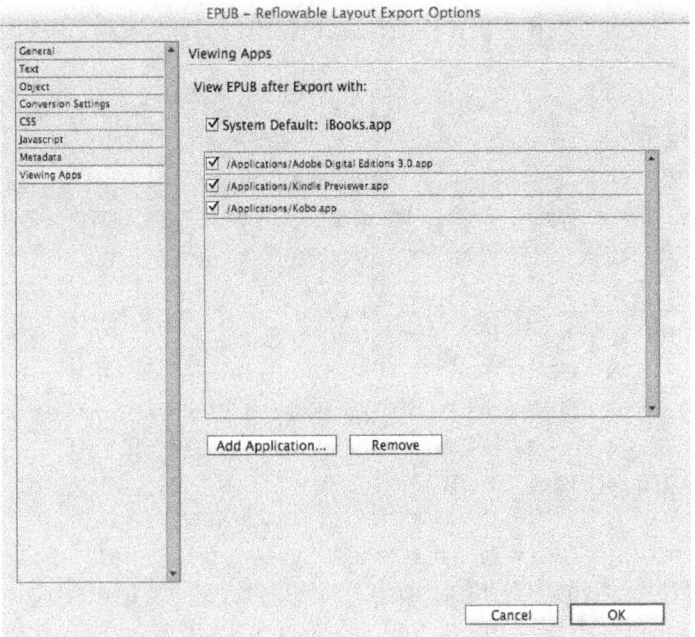

View after Exporting: Always check this. This has changed for me lately now that the fourth version of Adobe Digital Editions is out. But ADE4 is still inferior. Readium [requires Chrome] is fairly good. Now that iBooks is in OSX Mavericks or newer, that is the best option. Always look over the exported ePUB in ADE4 before you validate and upload. You also need to check in iBooks. Increasingly, I check it out in BlueFire on my iPad. I am still regularly surprised by something that needs to be fixed.

Always test with crappy ereaders: I have a tendency to only test in the ereaders which show everything. Quite regularly I am surprised and disgusted with what is actually displayed in Nook, Kobo, or the e-ink ereaders in general. Basically, that means you need to test using the apps on your iPad. You don't have an iPad? Then you don't really have to worry because you have crappy already well-defined by everything except Readium and Fire.

This is not a smooth process yet. It is really good that InDesign can now export ePUBs that can be validated. But it probably will not be uneventful until InDesign CCNext+2 or so. InDesign CC is getting pretty good, but there is still a long ways to go.

Click OK and you've got an ePUB

It will open in your reader of choice. Proof it carefully in a variety of ereading apps or hardware. Redo as necessary. You will quickly develop a good idea of what is translating well and what does not work for you. I need to reiterate: **proof carefully and often.** You need to go through every ePUB you export page by page. Adobe Digital Editions 4 is a problem. It will show fonts from your hard drive on your computer which will not show in your ereader. On the other hand, do not be seduced by iBooks. It's in another league. Most ereaders will not do nearly as well as you see in iBooks.

Validate it

Redo the proof as often as necessary. I used to suggest that you go to: http://validator.idpf.org/ for validation. But, I haven't had an ePUB which wouldn't validate for a long time with InDesign CC. I no longer worry about it. The exported ePUBs simply work.

Uploading to the various places

Before you even think of doing this make sure that you have the following under control.

🐄 The book's title

🐄 The book's subtitle (Optional)

- 🐪 The description
- 🐪 The price
- 🐪 The keywords

Without all of these things well in hand, the uploading process to the various suppliers will much more complicated than you want it to be. Plus, you will have a hard time being consistent. If you are not consistent, your book will be listed in various ways in various places. Your readers will be confused. Google will be confused. Amazon will be confused. You do not want that.

You formerly needed to make a special rasterization of your cover for each vendor. But both Kindle and D2D use the 2500px tall minimum. They all have different size requirements if you upload directly in each one. This is one of the main reasons I suggest you have your front cover separate in PDF form. That way each rasterization will be sharp and crisp. The only problem now is that the various covers have different proportions, which for which it can be a bear to adjust.

Never forget these are Web documents

Actually, as you know, they are not exactly that. There are many Web page possibilities which cannot be used in an ePUB. But, the basic capabilities are the same. You are using HTML and CSS with 72 dpi images a maximum of 600 pixels wide in almost all cases.

The major fly in the ointment

Amazon [thud]

Converting to Kindle

Again we are dealing with fixed layout [Print Replica], and reflowable [a normal Kindle book].

Kindle KDP has their own version (as usual) of a fixed layout ebook called Textbook or Print Replica. They give you free software, Kindle Textbook Creator, which starts by opening a PDF. It opens it; asks if you want to save the hyperlinks used (and you click yes), and then you package it. If you're paranoid, proof it carefully. But the PDF should be already proofed. Because there is no penalty for color, I use my downloadable PDF Version. The result is a converted PDF which Amazon calls a .kdf—it's an encapsulated PDF of some kind, and they're not telling.

The normal reflowable Kindle book

Until the summer of 2012, I gave some very explicit instructions for the construction of the HTML and CSS needed to step back in time to Amazon's MOBI format. It was extremely limited in what was allowed. It was all done by writing HTML by hand. Things have gotten a lot better. In fact, in many ways, Kindle's KF8 Export Plug-in for CS6 and earlier worked very well. You could export a Kindle book easily, though it was missing many capabilities.

Now with CC things have changed again. There was a short time period where Amazon's plug-in was doing better than converting an ePUB. This was also the same time frame where Amazon was bouncing all MOBIs made with non-Amazonian software. But now you can just upload your ePUB or convert it in Kindle Previewer.

Kindle Previewer 3.0

One of the less heralded features of Amazon's free Kindle Previewer is that is will do a good job of converting an ePUB using Kindle Gen. This was my production workflow until very recently [July, 2016].

☞ **First I export an ePUB with embedded fonts:** this is my upload for all my distributors.

☞ **Next I package the document used to create the ePUB into a new folder:** in the Amazon folder for the Kindle version.

☞ **In the newly packaged Links folder, I go through all the linked graphics:** [They are all JPEGs at 100% quality to avoid artifacts].

☞ **Any graphic which is over 125 KB needs to be resized:** I open the original into Photoshop and make a JPEG which is less than 120 KB. Amazon will re-rasterize anything not done this way, badly blur, and otherwise mess up your graphic. They do claim this step is no longer necessary. You try it, not me!

☞ **I use Save For Web to get the file size of the graphics adjusted to less than 120 KB:** A couple of times I have saved them at exactly 127 KB and Amazon still resized them—thereby ruining them.

☞ **If I do that, I Save As a PSD:** and save the original JPEG as a PSD in a new Originals folder.

☞ **Change all the object styles to your Inline option, flush left or centered:** The fancy anchored objects options are stripped out by Kindle—not uncommonly stripping out the entire graphic.

🐫 **When all the graphics are fixed, I export a new ePUB:** I open it in Kindle Previewer to convert it to a KF8 package for KDP uploads. I used Previewer to Proof.

🐫 **Kindle Previewer 3.0 [Beta] is what we use to see what the Kindle book looks like after we export the ePUB:** It uses KindleGen to convert the new CC ePUBs to KF8 books and then views them. However, if you use Fixed for the CSS Size the preview graphic sizes will be very small. I am told that this is not an issue once the book is viewed in your Kindle. But I don't have one.

It worked for a couple of years. I stuck with the procedure for a long time. But I keep seeing horrible things in Previewer's proof. Basically, previewer doesn't work well on a Mac. You cannot trust the proof.

The problem is all the different models of Kindle sold by Amazon. They all have radically different capabilities. But the strange thing is that Previewer was (and is) messing up my books horribly.

I discovered several problems by examining KDP's Formatting Guide in detail. I found some real horrors:

🐫 **1. Page Size**

1 to 1.6 ratio: 5"x8"; 600x960; 6"x9.6" for Print Replica

Image resolution

🐫 **1200px by 1920px @ 300 dpi:** Yes! This is what they now recommend.

I quote: "**Images should maintain a 1920 x 1200 aspect ratio:** The image resolution will differ depending on the zoom factor required for Kindle Panel View. However, Amazon recommends planning for a high quality reading experience at 2X magnification. Images must be in the JPEG format. Amazon recommends using an image resolution of 300 ppi."

There you have it—a radical change indeed.

Body Copy

☞"Body text must use the default font size (1em) and line height. Body text should not use the <font size="…"> tag or the font-size and line-height attributes in CSS. "

As far as I can tell, It sounds like body copy must be formatted as [Basic Paragraph]. This would include all styles based on body copy also.

☞"Body text must not have an imposed left/right margin or padding throughout the book: If there are paragraphs that do require left/right margin to differentiate them visually from body text, like a recipe list or a block quote, margins applied to these sections should be specified as percentages rather than ems or point values."

☞"Kindle Reader does not honor line-height value less than 1.2 em or 120%:"

To translate, heads and subheads are going to be horribly spaced at HTML defaults. Although we can be optimistic and assume that this is only talking about body copy and its derivatives. Headline [h1] is normally set solid, or 1 em 100%.

☞"Margins should be assigned values of 0 or greater to keep content from falling off the edge of the screen or overlapping other content:"

Always set left and right margins to 0 for normal body text to allow users the full range of margin selection using device defaults. Top/bottom margins should be specified in ems so that spacing between paragraphs is easily distinguishable at any font or device size."

Table design

📷"For the best user experience, tables should not contain whole paragraphs of text or large pictures in a cell."

Translation: If you have a fancy table, save it as a PDF, rasterize that PDF in Photoshop at 300dpi. Then Save As a GIF or PNG. JPEGs tend to blur rasterized type and linework.

📷 If a table is too large or contains too much text in its cells, consider reformatting it in a way that maintains legible text: Single columns of HTML text provide the best reading experience for customers using a variety of font sizes.

📷 Optimize tables to be no larger than 10 Kindle screens: A Kindle screen is approximately 24 rows of 60 characters, although the Kindle DX shows more characters. The character limit is the maximum number of characters in any one row.

Translation: Any table over 60 characters wide needs to be converted to a graphic as described above. In general, between border and fill controls, graphic cells [new for CC2015.4}, and type, ALL tables need to be rasterized.

📷 All lowercase characters must be at least 6 pixels tall

Translation: the x-height after rasterization must be 6 pixels at a minimum.

Images

Basically, nothing is changed here. For CS6 and earlier, I still recommend that you place all images inline. For CC ePUBs, all images are changed into anchored objects. Kindle Previewer or the direct KDP upload seem to strip out a lot of that information.

Quality issues with the Kindle books still remain very frustrating. I imagine it is much easier to deal with if you have a Fire.

The Kindle supports GIF, BMP, JPEG, PNG images in your content. Vector graphics are not supported and must be converted to raster graphics. **The size limit for images is 127KB [120KB actual].** Below this limit, all images will be exported unaltered. While above this limit, images will be automatically optimized [re-rasterized] to be under the size limit during conversion. You should understand this to mean that images larger than 125KB will be ruined. That is straight forward enough. But then, what do we do with the encouraged preference of 300dpi images?

Here's another warning from Amazon about images with text:

I'll just quote them on this also:

For images containing a lot of text, using the GIF format is recommended so that the sharpness and legibility of the text is retained. Since an image is always displayed completely on the screen, image resolution should be constrained to a maximum of 500x600 [ed: 600w x 500h] so that the image is not scaled, making it hard to read.

Minimum font size should be such that a lower-case "a" is at least 6 pixels tall. You can reduce the number of colors used in an image to optimize its size or split the image horizontally to keep it under the size limit. It is highly recommended that automatic optimization by KindleGen be avoided in case of images containing text.

My recommendation is that you do what you need to do to entirely avoid any "optimization" by making your images smaller than 125K and 600 pixels wide or narrower. Notice they specify that images larger than 600x500 pixels will be scaled. This means that you need to keep the height less than 500 pixels also.

Changes in image resolution: I will be experimenting and will share those experiments with *The Skilled Workman [TSW]*. Setting up the Object panel, as we did for reflow ePUBs, results in quite small images in Kindle Previewer. I'll see if they get any better in the KDP Preview.

My guess is that I'll be using the highest resolution I have—in most cases they are screen captures, so they'll be 72 dpi. But at least I won't have to make them smaller, as I do now. I'll try my full resolution images at 300 dpi. But I'd be surprised if I can do that—simply because the file size will rapidly go over the 50 MB limit. Like I said, I'll keep you apprised in TSW.

Cover image

It's required and it needs to be exactly 600x800. In the past JPEGs were virtually required. I found that unless they were produced by Photoshop's Save for Web command I had troubles. I set up my images exactly to spec before placing them into my InDesign document.

The KDP upload process will have you upload the cover image again in addition to the one embedded in your book, for their use. Their exact recommendation, for this marketing cover image, is 1563 pixels by 2500 pixels. It's all pretty straight forward. The KDP Publishing guidelines are linked off the plug-in page. My basic design recommendations remain the same as we discussed for ePUBs, modified only by what you see above.

Bottomline on the Kindle Export Plug-In & Previewer

Since the summer of 2012, everything I've exported with the new plug-in worked as expected and has been accepted by KDP. Then I used Kindle Previewer—which also worked well. I uploaded the CC ePUBs directly in KDP last year. I went back to using Kindle Previewer 3.0. Now I am uploading the heavily modified CC ePUBs without embedded fonts directly in KDP.

No embedded fonts? That's right!

When checking out the conversions in Kindle Previewer, I found that each level of quality had a different result. Strangely, the Fire and Fire HDX both stripped out all the font information. As far as I can tell, it has to do with there new Enhanced Typography. That conversion to Bookerly eliminates all embedded fonts—but that's simply a guess.

 Remember, I mentioned that this Enhanced Typography is added after uploading—completely outside your control: Evidently, stripping the fonts is required to make the Bookerly conversion go smoothly. You'll never see it unless you buy a copy of your own book.

Dealing with lists

Nothing but normal HTML lists with a regular bullet work at all. They may be horribly ugly—but nothing nearly as bad as what you see after they chew up your beautiful lists which were converted to text. So, this is another change in the export.

Our conclusions?

Book quality in Kindle is still a problem and will remain so until they give us tools and instructions which cover their "better typography". Supposedly you can now use much larger images, as mentioned. I'm not willing to risk that. If I come up with a new and better procedure, I'll keep you up to date on *The Skilled Workman*. The big thing to remember is that the fancy features only work in the Fire, several only in Fire HD and HDX. And that Kindle Previewer or the KDP upload chews up most of them also.

Dealing with the old e-ink Kindles, Nooks, & Kobos

These remain popular and for graphic designers, this is horrible news. All anchored object stying is stripped out and the images are placed inline, on their own line, flush left. All font information is stripped out—including the serif and sans serif distinctions. I would be concerned about much more. Tables are dumped or rasterized by them [no, you do not want that]! The only borders kept are those rasterized within the Photoshop images. These e-ink ereaders are very much like reading your book in NotePad or TextEdit. The thought makes me nauseous.

However, the users of these devices usually read nothing but novels. Novels are very simple books. So, these issues are not nearly as bad as they seem.

The Kindle bottomline?

You need a new version with many changes. I just covered most of them. But proof carefully. I'm finding new problems all the time. Any Kindle conversion not done from Word in their own laboratories is suspect and dealt with harshly.

This is the only instance I know of where it might just be better if you hire a HTML/CSS design specialist to code the entire book by hand in an HTML editor. I've never done that, though.

Horrors!

However, if you make the changes I suggested: do not embed fonts, use simple lists, rasterize tables, and the list goes on and on, then your Kindle books will look fairly good—and far better than the ones done by Amazon in-house from poorly structured Word docs. They are Amazon's true problem in KDP. A professionally designed book is outside that entire paradigm.

Your book may be brutalized by the Enhanced Typography, but if your structure is good, it will remain. That's what will keep your Kindle books looking good.

Colophon:

This book has been written in my small office at the back of our 132 year old [1881], two-story framed home in southern Minnesota—Mankato to be specific: It is a beautiful old section of this small city with streets lined with large, mature trees, brick and framed two and three story homes, near the bottom of the large (200–300 foot) bluffs lining the Minnesota River valley in this area. This is part of the view through the window next to my built-in desk. Actually it was the view in August 2013.

I have a 21.5" late 2013 iMac, running El Capitan, with 16gb ram, an old Epson scanner, and cable modem access to the Web. I'm using Adobe's InDesign CC 2015.4 for this book along with the latest update to Photoshop CC 2015.5, as of last week.

For the fonts, I designed the basic fonts used in this book in FontLab 5—though these fonts were designed for my new book on font design using Fontographer 5.1. The fonts were designed as part of my personal best seller, *Practical Font Design With FontLab 5*. The serif faces are from the four-font Librum family and the headers are from the companion font family I designed for Librum: Librum Sans. For ePUBs, I use a special ebook font family named, Librium E which I also designed.

I produced all the graphics as well, though there are several royalty-free photos scattered in the book. The captures were mainly done with Snapz Pro X, though I used GrabIt for timed captures, and the Finder shortcuts when it didn't matter.

As usual, it has been great fun putting this book together for you. I pray it's helpful for you in your work.

Today, it's a warm and wet day in September. This weekend promises to feel like Fall. Gorgeous weather—down to 50° tonight. I'm going out to work in the garden for a while.

Thank you for reading the book. Please review it, especially if you liked it.

Friday, September 9, 2016
Mankato, Minnesota

My online addresses:

My technical blog: http://bergsland.org
My Christian blog: http://radiqx.com
My normal email: david@radiqx.com

FaceBook: https://www.facebook.com/radiqxpress
Pinterest: http://www.pinterest.com/radiqxpress/
Gumroad: https://gumroad.com/radiqxpress
Twitter [Christian]: @radiqxpress
Twitter [technical]: @davidbergsland
Google+: +DavidBergsland

Book availability

Search for David Bergsland for the books listed on the bookstore site you prefer. Almost all of my books are on Amazon [Kindle & print], Nook, the iBooks Store, Kobo, Smashwords, Scribd, and many other locations where the various distributors having gotten the books listed.

I have an author page on Amazon, and a great deal of information in both of my Website/blogs.

Thank you for reading my book,